Sock Architecture

Heels, Toes & Techniques
for Knitting Awesome Socks

LARA NEEL

Sock Architecture

Library of Congress Control Number: 2014947579
ISBN 13 (print): 978-1-937513-63-4
ISBN 13 (e-book): 978-1-937513-64-1
First Edition
Published by Cooperative Press
www.cooperativepress.com

Every effort has been made to ensure that all the information in this book is accurate at the time of publication. Cooperative Press neither endorses nor guarantees the content of external links referenced in this book. All business names, trademarks and product names used within the text are the property of their respective owners. If you have questions or comments about this book, or need information about licensing, custom editions, special sales, or academic/corporate purchases, please contact Cooperative Press: info@cooperativepress.com or 13000 Athens Ave C288, Lakewood, OH 44107 USA

COOPERATIVE PRESS

Senior Editor: Shannon Okey
Acquisitions Editor / Assistant Editor: MK Carroll
Art Director / Assistant Editor: Elizabeth Green Musselman
Technical Editors: Kate Atherley and Eleanor Dixon

For my Nana, who didn't have the
chance to write her books.

Table of Contents

Techniques

Patterns

STRIE,
TOP DOWN [50]

STRIE,
TOE UP [54]

MOUCHOIR,
TOP DOWN [58]

MOUCHOIR,
TOE UP [62]

CHECKED & SQUARE,
TOP DOWN [66]

CHECKED & SQUARE,
TOE UP [72]

BOOTSTRAP [76]

UNCOMMON
DRAGON [80]

DYAD,
TOP DOWN [86]

DYAD,
TOE UP [92]

PROCRASTINATRIX,
TOP DOWN [98]

PROCRASTINATRIX,
TOE UP [102]

SIDLE,
TOP DOWN [106]

SIDLE,
TOE UP [110]

ARITHMOPHOBIA,
TOP DOWN [114]

ARITHMOPHOBIA,
TOE UP [118]

ADJOIN [122]

Resources

Techniques
Techniques
Techniques
Techniques
Techniques
Techniques

I FIRST LEARNED HOW TO knit (but not purl, cast on or cast off) at daycare when I was about five or six years old. After I left that particular daycare, there was no one to help me start or stop my knitting, so I simply stopped. I blame the acrylic yarn I was using—surely wool fumes would have made my conversion into a knitter more permanent.

When I was in college, around 1998, I decided to relearn knitting. So, I tracked down every single book I could find about knitting, pored over woolworks.org and read the KnitList. I remember making a very small shawl because I didn't understand gauge yet and a few pairs of worsted-weight cotton socks that my aunt still remembers because "you knit a whole sock just during graduation!" It was really just the foot of a sock, since they were meant to be worn like old-fashioned tennis socks, but I let her be impressed anyway.

Those socks marked the first time I customized a sock to fit a particular foot. My identical twin sister has an extra bit of bone on the back of her left heel. When I turned the short-row heel for her, I added more shaping so that it would fit her well.

Years later, I met the love of my life. I don't remember if she asked me for hand-knit socks or if I offered them. But her job required her to be on her darling, tiny feet all of the time, and I had heard that bamboo fiber content in socks can make working feet feel less tired, so I cast on.

She loved her new socks, and soon I was knitting all-wool ones, too, to defeat the cold of South Dakota winters.

After our move to Indiana, I helped start the Crafty Living blog at my new newspaper, *The Journal Gazette*. For the blog, I restarted my podcast, Math4Knitters <math4knitters.blogspot.com>, but also wrote book reviews every Friday for a long time.

In the midst of a spate of sock-knitting book reviews, I happened to look at the cover of *The Knitter's Book of Socks* by Clara Parkes upside-down and kind of sideways. The Stepping Stones sock photo caught my eye and I thought, "Why *not* knit a flap-and-gusset heel sideways?"

I spent that Friday night and Saturday morning trying it, and brought the result to my friend and yarn shop owner extraordinaire Allison Van Zandt at Simply Socks Yarn Company <simplysockyarn.com>, which is right around the corner from my house. She encouraged me to write it up and submit it to Knitty. I did, and just about died of excitement when my Tootsie sock pattern was accepted for their Spring + Summer 2012 edition <knitty.com/ISSUEss12/PATTtootsie.php>.

My twin sister modeled the socks in Allison's store for the magazine. If you look very closely at some of the photos, you can see her unique foot shape. (This time, her heel didn't matter; socks knit at a finer gauge are more forgiving, as you'll see.)

Some time later, another knitting friend expressed frustration at not being able to figure out what kind of heels and toes would best fit different members of her family. I told her I could write up a chart. I then spent several weeks obsessively hunting down heel and toe shapes, reading about feet, doodling, and typing it all up.

The result is this book. I hope you enjoy it half as much as did I.

Introduction

East, West, and a Little History

1

CURRENTLY, MOST socks are designed to be worked as straight tubes through the foot, with a brief bit of shaping for the heel, and also straight, with maybe a little shaping, to the top of the sock's leg. Historically, there was a lot more shaping throughout the foot—and the relationship between the heel, especially, and the rest of the sock could be very different.

In *A History of Handknitting*, Richard Rutt divides sock knitting neatly into two categories: Eastern and Western. He notes that Western knitting encourages socks that have horizontal bands of patterning and that are worked top-down using with four needles. Eastern-style socks tend to be divided between the front and back, have vertical patterning, are worked with five needles, and are toe-up. These distinctions generally still hold today, except for the number of needles and in parts of the world where both influences are felt (Rutt, p. 210).

Traditional Western-style socks are knit from the top down, with a flap-and-gusset heel and a toe that ends in grafting. There is nearly always a gusset with this style of sock. However, as you shall see, all of these design elements can be changed to suit a particular style and fit, and a gusset isn't always needed.

Rutt writes that in Eastern socks, toes and heels are triangular pouches (p. 218). This is true, but there is a lot more to it than that. Eastern-style socks lend themselves to interesting stitch pattern treatments and tend to have heels and toes that are easy to work and, if they develop holes, easy to replace. They may not be a traditional style in all areas, but I include short-row toes and heels among Eastern sock constructions, because they don't use a gusset.

Eastern-style socks are made from the toe up, often start with a seamless cast on, and proceed straight through the top of the leg. Stitches for the heel are picked up and worked after the rest of the sock is complete. For this reason, they are often called "afterthought" heels.

In a caption to a photo in her book *Ethnic Socks & Stockings: A Compendium of Eastern Design and Technique*, Priscilla Gibson-Roberts asserts that, even though Western and Eastern styles look very different, "the differences fade when the socks are worn" (p. 12).

While that may generally be true, I feel I should share a small warning with knitters unfamiliar with the Eastern style of sock. They can be hard to pull on. Some children's versions that I have seen photographed in museum collections have open tops, with ties to close the leg of the sock. This may be because a stiff, colorwork-rich, Eastern-style sock could be nearly impossible to put on a squirming toddler without this option. However, Anna Zilboorg reports that, once on, the socks are incredibly warm and worth the effort, both in knitting and wearing (p. 8)!

Many knitters think they don't like afterthought or short-row heels because the fit in most patterns isn't customized. Narrow feet with high arches, in particular, are badly suited to the average short-row or afterthought heel. Fortunately, we don't have to stick to averages, and a customized toe-up sock design can even include a gusset. If you have avoided afterthought heels because you think they are too shallow, at least consider trying a thumb-joint afterthought heel. It is deeper and, in my experience, fits very well to the foot.

If you really want to follow in Rutt's footsteps, you can check out his library online, for free: <southampton.ac.uk/library/ldu/wsa.html>.

Inspiration from the Museum

In the process of research for this book (and just general tooling around), I've looked at a lot of socks from museum collections. I find them fascinating. I haven't been able to incorporate every design detail from my wanderings into my patterns, yet, so I'll just point out some that any ambitious knitter could add for themselves.

1) Color changes in less-than-usual places.
Some of my favorite examples of colorwork occupy just a very small part of the sock: the turn of the heel, the tip of the toe, a two-color cast on. Maybe one day I'll even get over my fear of intarsia and do a very deep clock panel in a contrasting color. Sometimes there's just a little color patterning to set off the gusset and I think it is so cute. Several machine-made stockings in museum collections have a contrast color just for the stitched seams at the heel and toe. It could have been because they didn't have a matching thread, but it is rather striking.

If you want to have a contrasting color just at the turn of the heel, you might want an extra row of that color right at the junction between the heel flap and the heel turn. For a toe-up sock, the extra row of contrasting color would be needed for the first row/round of the heel flap (or, possibly, the pickup/setup round for the heel flap). For a top-down sock, the extra row would be the last row of the heel flap.

I've worked this patch of color both with and without that extra row. In my opinion, it doesn't look that different, and the extra-row version had two more ends to darn in. The knitter will know her or his own preferences.

2) Pattern stitch extending to a part of the sock foot that is normally just stockinette.
You have to be a little careful here. No one wants to step on lace or cables. My foot, for example, is 8½ inches around at the ball of my foot, so I like my socks to have a circumference of about 7¾ inches, but the part of my foot that actually touches the ground is only 3½ inches across. About 4¼ inches of my sock foot could be worked in a pattern, as long as it wasn't so bulky I wouldn't be able to wear shoes. Careful measurement and probably a good-sized gauge swatch would be needed, but it would be a fun customization to any sock.

3) One pattern of colorwork on the sole, and another on the top of the sock.
This is especially common on lovely Eastern-style socks.

4) Embroidery, anywhere and everywhere.
I suppose a real wimp like me could start with just a tiny lazy daisy on the back of the leg, and go from there … or cross-stitch an initial. I'm also very much in love with a pair of stockings from the Museum of Fine Arts in Boston <mfa.org/collections/object/pair-of-stockings-65720>. Exactly one column of lace patterning on the side of the white leg is outlined in red.

5) Combination of stripes that run in different directions.
There is a nineteenth-century French pair from the Met that I swear could be on the runway today. <bit.ly/1Ol8Ogx>

The Names of Things, and the Rise of the Round (French) Heel

Having taken some inspiration from historical sock knitting, let's take a closer look at one specific issue in the sock's history: namely, why a certain kind of rounded heel became so popular in Western knitting.

To return to Richard Rutt, cut-and-sewn, woven cloth stockings continued to be worn for a long time after knitting was introduced to Europe, especially by the upper classes. This is a bit mystifying to modern knitters. The stretch and fit inherent to knit fabric is so wonderful that modern-day clothiers use it for nearly everything. T-shirts, underpants, and even some bedsheets are made of stretchy, smooshy knit

---

Fashion's capacity to cling for centuries to a decorative element that no longer serves a purpose is remarkable. Consider the case of the little buttons near the sleeve of a man's dress jacket. They are pointless, right? Well, they always were. They are simply there as decoration, a holdover from the 1650s when people were just so super excited that they could even have buttons that they couldn't stand it and put them all over everything (Bryson, location 6634).

Why is the round heel so ubiquitous, at least in English-language knitting instructions? Why is it called the French heel? I don't know the answer to either question, but that doesn't keep me from forming theories. The common heel's name, by the way, is easy to figure out. A glance at a museum collection of stockings shows that is was very, very widely used, especially for machine-knit and cloth stockings. I have the giant Pinterest board to prove it, too: <pinterest.com/laran/knitspiration/>.

fabric. Look closely: I promise that nearly every stretchy fabric in your life is made of teeny-tiny knit stitches.

But old habits die hard, not least because good-quality knitting needles were hard to come by for a long time in Europe (Rutt, p. 62).

Even after knit stockings—even machine-made knit stockings—became the norm, a lot of style cues, seam placements, and shaping techniques appeared to imitate the fit, cut and look of cloth hose. For example, consider the decorative stitching on the sides of many cloth hose, called clocks. They were originally meant to hide a side seam. Some of them involved incredibly elaborate feats of embroidery and were certainly very pretty. They persisted as decoration on knit socks and stockings for a very long time, indeed, even though they served no practical purpose.

So how did the rounded heel that we now associate with knitted socks come into being, and why is that shaping called French? To understand, we need to know a little about some of the early heel shapes.

"Common" heels are rarely seen today, but they were quite common, indeed, when the name was first given to them by knitting writers of the day. Common heels can be machine-made or knit by hand, and require either a seam or grafting on the bottom of the heel to close them.

Round heels are heels that are turned with a series of short rows that are shorter at the back of the heel and longer toward the sole of the foot. Their "round" shape is formed by the short rows, in fact.

Now let's look at how such heels came to be called French.

THEORY 1: BLAME IT ON THE VICTORIANS. WHY NOT?

At roughly the start of the Victorian era, knitting became an acceptable diversion for ladies, not just a way for members of the lower classes to avoid starvation. The first books of printed instructions for knitting patterns in English were published at that time (Rutt, p. 111). Executing the round heel takes a little know-how, but no grafting, and it is clearly not machine-made. It may have been preferred over the common heel for those reasons. Also, if the directions are written well, it doesn't take a lot of space to explain. (I should note that brevity and clarity were both rare in early knitting patterns, so this just may help explain why the round heel has remained the most widely used, but not how it got that way.)

In her *Lady's Assistant for Executing Useful and Fancy Designs in Knitting, Netting, and Crochet Work*, Jane Gaugain included several patterns for stockings and seems like a good person to blame the "French" heel on. Alas for that theory, all of the patterns for stockings in that book have shaped common heels, not round ones. *Exercises in Knitting* points to its author, Cornelia Mee, as another possible culprit. But she never uses the term French heel and appears to include a square heel turn for her stocking.

The first instructions I can find that explicitly link a French heel with round heel shaping is from 1870. In *The Stocking-Knitter's Manual: A Handy Book for the Work-Table*, Mrs. George Cupples lists a French (round), Dutch (square) and Common heel. Her instructions for the Common heel complain that the seam can be uncomfortable (Cupples, p. 6). It's a good thing that we modern knitters can graft the heel closed, to avoid such problems.

Cupples also suggests a different way to work a heel when the recipient has a "high instep or a stout foot." It's quite interesting. The heel is worked over about 10 percent fewer stitches than normal (those 10 percent are left on the instep). After the turn, 6 stitches are added to the back of the foot before gusset decreases begin. Gusset decreases stop when the foot has 10 percent more stitches than before heel shaping began.

THEORY 2: A FRENCH WRITER INVENTED IT, OR MAYBE WROTE IT DOWN FIRST.

The first round heel shaping I could find was written by Madamoiselle Riego de la Branchardiere in 1867, whom Rutt describes as a rival to Mrs. Mee (p. 116). In *The Abergeldie Winter Book*, Branchardiere gives instructions on how to "Round the Heel." (p. 12) It's a lovely book, too, with wonderful components the modern reader will appreciate like illustrations, paragraph breaks and subheadings.

According to a contemporary biographer, Branchardiere's father was French (Rutt, p. 116). Perhaps she wrote either the first version or the first widely available version of this heel, and people attached "French" to it because of her.

THEORY 3: "FRENCH" JUST SOUNDS MORE SOPHISTICATED TO US ANGLOPHONES.

After all, it is a marketing term today that is still used to sell high-end products, especially makeup and perfume. Why not sock heel turns?

AS KNITTING HAS developed, more and more types of sock construction have developed, leading the modern knitter to wonder, "How do I best knit socks to fit my own foot?"

We are used to thinking about fit and sizing in absolute terms, but you only have to look at the variety of shapes available in jeans to see that fit is as much a function of style as it is a representation of exacting physical measurements. With that said, certain styles of heels and toes in socks will fit different sorts of feet with more or less comfort. In this chapter, I will help you work out what works best for your foot, shoes, and lifestyle. To do this, I'm breaking away from the traditional division between "Eastern" and "Western" styles and instead focusing on the direction of the knitting—from toe up or top down. Using this structure, the knitter can choose the style of heel or toe that suits their needs best.

Of course, we could avoid the fit problem altogether by making socks entirely without heels or toes. In the past, these garments have been called "hoggers" or gaiters (Rutt, p. 64), but we would call them leg warmers. In some ways, they are very practical, in that sizing is almost a moot issue, and there is nothing to rub against a shoe and wear out. On the other hand, they won't keep your feet warm all by themselves.

For a long time, most sock patterns were written in a general way, for a specific size, or with suggestions for changing the length of the foot to determine the size. Many patterns are still that way, but a lot of designers are writing patterns with changes in both length and width, to allow for a more exacting fit. When choosing someone else's sock pattern, read it carefully to see which kind of sizing you are dealing with.

No matter what style of sock you want, careful measurements are needed to get a great-fitting sock. The bare minimum measurements are listed on the next page. Please take notes when you knit your first sock, so that you can make the second sock exactly alike.

If you are making socks for someone else and think you might, at some point in the future, make another set of socks for them, it makes sense to save measuring time and keep your notes. I seem to always leave my notes in my other knitting bag. So I've made a digital copy of this person's sock measurements and fit preferences. It resides online in a few places, where I hope I can always get them if I am trapped in, say, an airport with a lot of time on my hands and nothing but emergency sock knitting to do. It's not a perfect solution, but I like it a lot better than trying to remember or count (from a sock that is already on the recipient's foot) how many stitches I cast on last time. The unwillingness of ungrateful non-knitters to take off their shoe in a public place so I can examine socks that I made will always be a mystery to me.

If you like, you could use the note section on page 12 to make your own template for future socks. You might want to note, especially, your measurements and calculations in a completely unrounded way. For example, if your sock is 7.2 inches around at 9 sts/inch, you would want 64.8 sts for your sock. That's impossible, of course. But, I like to write it down so that I know, if I need to round up or down for a stitch count, which way I should err. I should really just cast on 65 sts, but I might need an even number and go for 64 sts. If I'm nervous that my gauge might actually be 9.25 sts/in with this yarn, it might be wiser to go for 66 sts. Again, experience is the best guide, but keeping good notes never hurt, either.

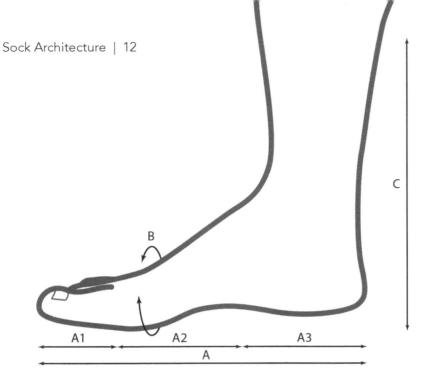

My Foot Measurements

Length of foot (A)	
Length of sock's foot—multiply A × 0.9 to get a good standard length of 10% smaller than the foot	
The length of the sock foot can then be divided into: • Length of heel (and gusset) shaping (A3) • Length of straight portion of sock foot (A2) • Length of toe shaping (A1) *For toe-up socks, measure A1 and calculate A3. For top-down socks, measure A3 and calculate A1. For all of them: A2 = A − (A1 + A3). Don't panic! Calculated sections will be proportional to the stitch count of the sock. Instructions for specific socks will include information on how to do it.*	
Circumference around ball of foot or widest area near the toes (B)	
Circumference of sock— multiply B ×0.9 to get a good standard circumference of 10% smaller than your foot circumference *This, times stitch gauge, is the circumference of the sock, in stitches. I will refer to the number of stitches needed to create this circumference as S throughout the text. You may need to round up or down to make S make sense for your stitch pattern. If you do, always double-check to make sure you haven't decided to make a sock that is widely different from the measurement of the foot. (More than 15% would be a large difference.)*	
Length of sock leg, from floor to top (C)	

Foot Shapes

Feet are as unique as faces. Even identical twins may have slightly different feet because of weight changes, shoe style preference, and physical activities. (Ask me how I know.)

Most people's toes fit into one of three categories: tapered, rounded (the second toe can be longer than or the same length as the big toe), or square.

"Tapered" means that a line drawn from the big toe to the little toe forms a nearly straight, sloped line. This is sometimes called an "Egyptian" foot.

When the second toe is longer than the big toe—and this is pretty much only possible with an otherwise rounded shape—this is called a "Grecian" foot.

I've noticed that people with a square toe shape (sometimes called "peasant" feet) are often self-conscious about their toes. According to an article in *Dance Magazine* <dancemagazine.com/issues/March-2008/If-The--Shoe-Fits> (and who thinks more about feet than dancers, really) the ball of the foot is wider than usual in comparison to the heel and "street shoes may be difficult to fit."

Knitters to the rescue! Everyone deserves socks that fit well. Hand-knit socks, since they are thicker than most commercially available ones, may even reduce fit problems that some people have with shoes. In particular, both of the square-footed people I know wear shoes that are too long for them, and hand-knit socks keep the darn things on their feet.

The arches of the feet aren't discussed a lot in sock design, but the relationship between arches and the shape of the heel of the sock can matter. Arches are described as high, average, or flat. People with either flat feet or high arches normally know all about it because they can have trouble finding shoes that are comfortable. If you have a high arch, a sock design that isn't generous enough through the gusset and heel will annoy you a great deal. It's possible to have a high instep but flat feet. This shape of foot also benefits from more room through the gusset and heel.

If you aren't sure which kind of arch shape you have, try the "wet foot" test. Wet your foot, then stand on something flat and dry. The concrete around a pool is great for this. Can you see the outline of your entire foot in your wet foot print? You have pretty flat feet. Are only the ball of your foot and the heel really visible? Those are high-arched feet.

A lot of the way sock heels are designed seems to be meant to deal with shoe style and wear, rather than an exact physical match to the heel of the foot. The style, fit, and shape of the shoes you wear might affect your socks. Ease of knitting and aesthetic considerations can sometimes take the forefront, assuming you are choosing between two heel styles that are equally durable and comfortable.

Choosing the best heel and toe shapes for your socks is discussed in more detail later. For now, see the sidebar at right for a down-and-dirty cheat sheet of heels and toes that might work best for you.

For much more about fitting your particular feet and legs, see Andi Smith's *Big Foot Knits*.

TESTING FOR FIT

I don't want to knit an entire sock, much less a pair of socks, just to see if I like the fit of an extra-long heel flap or a short-row toe. So, when I'm designing a custom-fit sock from scratch, I often knit sample pieces of the parts of the sock I am most interested in. For a heel, I cast on with a provisional cast on, work for about an inch in stockinette, then make the heel I am considering. I knit for another inch, then

place the live stitches on waste yarn. For a toe, I make the toe I am trying with about an inch of stockinette either before or after I make it, depending on which direction I am planning to knit the sock. These little test pieces are great for double-checking gauge and fit of the final piece. (You'll see many of my toe and heel "swatches" pictured throughout this book.) For sock toes, I can also measure exactly how long that particular toe is when knit in my yarn with my needles and my hands. Row gauge is tricky, so this is sometimes the only way to be sure of a new-to-me toe.

The ambitious or Kitchener-loving knitter could even use test pieces like these as starting points for socks. Either pick up where you left off or graft the test piece to the "real" sock. Or, just use up odds and ends of sock yarn to explore new techniques and end up with a weird-looking sock yarn drawer like mine.

Gauge, Fabric and Fit

If you want your socks to be comfortable and durable, use the smallest knitting needle size you and the yarn can stand. The leg of any sock can be subtly shaped by using a slightly larger needle, but that is entirely up to you. If you do change needles halfway through, make a note of it and make sure not to get two sets of needles mixed up with each other. It can be very frustrating to find that you have made one sock foot on one size needle and the other sock foot on a different size.

Most knitters end up with a different gauge when working back-and-forth (as for a heel flap) than when working in the round (for most of the rest of the sock). This is because many people purl more loosely than they knit. If you notice that this is a problem, you might try using a smaller needle on rows with a lot of purl stitches.

HEEL SHAPE SUGGESTIONS

High arches: Flap-and-Gusset Heels, Thumb-Joint Afterthought Heels, Afterthought Heels with Gussets

Average arches: Any heel, you lucky thing!

Low arches: Afterthought Heels, Short-Row Heels

TOE SHAPE SUGGESTIONS

Tapered: Long Wedge Toe, Long Sideways Toe, Narrow Short-Row Toe

Rounded: Medium Wedge Toe, Medium Sideways Toe, Round Toe, Swirl Toe, Medium Short-Row Toe

Square: Short Wedge Toe, Short Sideways Toe, Wide Short-Row Toe

To avoid this problem of too-loose purl stitches throwing off your gauge, make your gauge swatch in the round. If you don't want to cast on as many stitches as are needed for the sock for your swatch, cast on half as many, and make a swatch on double-pointed needles. Work all of the stitches, then slide the work from one end of the needle to the other, and start again at the beginning of the row/round. This makes a swatch that is fast and lies fairly flat. Take the swatch off the needles and measure gauge carefully while on a flat surface. The back will look very messy, but that is the price paid to save a little time. (See Working a Gauge Swatch "in the Round," page 14.)

Many knitters simply use the first few inches of sock in a top-down sock as a gauge swatch. I'm not going to

WORKING A GAUGE SWATCH "IN THE ROUND"

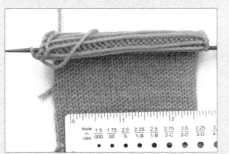 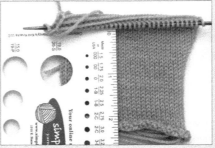 

say this doesn't work well, but if you have any doubts at all about matching the called-for gauge of a pattern, this takes up at least twice as much time as working a gauge swatch on half as many stitches.

The thinner the yarn and fabric, the more easily a sock will conform to the foot. Tights, which usually have no heel shaping at all, fit as well as they do because they are very thin and stretchy.

Ease is also a very important element of fit in socks. Usually, we talk about ease in terms of adding width to a garment, so that it won't be skin tight. Unlike many sweaters, socks should conform to the foot, so we actually use "negative ease" in sock design. Socks should be both narrower and shorter than the foot they should fit. Usually, about 10% of negative ease is needed (which only means that the sock should be 10% shorter and smaller around than the foot it is designed to fit). But, this will change depending on the flexibility and thickness of the fabric in the sock. Some stitch patterns and yarns are more inelastic than others, and might need special considerations for sizing.

If you are knitting socks for a gift, and can't measure the recipient, check out *The Knitter's Book of Socks* by Clara Parkes. The tables on pages 191–193 should be a good place to start.

ROUND GAUGE WOES

Round gauge is, at best, tricky. At worst it is downright maddening. Since socks are knit on smaller needles and with a tighter stitch gauge than most projects, round gauge can behave in a way that is difficult to predict. Colorwork and slipped stitches, in particular, can completely throw the usual rules about the relationship between stitch and round gauge out the window. Throughout this text, I will point out areas where this problem is especially acute. When in doubt, a swatch on *your* needles with *your* yarn and worked in the pattern stitch required is the only real way to check your gauge.

CALLING IN REINFORCEMENT

Traditionally, sock yarns were made simply of tightly plied wool. To toughen the toes and heels, some knitters added a reinforcement thread, usually made of nylon (or sometimes silk, especially before artificial fabrics came along), which was simply knit along with the working yarn for the toe and heel areas. There is some debate about if this actually makes socks last longer, however, and if you aren't using an easy-to-match color for your main yarn, finding a nylon thread to match can be difficult.

Fortunately, a lot of modern yarns designed for socks include some percentage of nylon, which does seem to help them last longer. The Simply Sock Yarn Solids that I used for this book is made up of 20% nylon and 80% wool. It wears very, very well.

There's nothing wrong with knitting socks out of pure, 100% wool yarn. But, the cautious knitter will either learn to love darning or use techniques to make the toes and heels of their nylon-free socks as tough as possible.

A simple way to increase the strength of any bit of knitting is to double the thickness of the yarn used. That is, work with two strands of yarn held together, instead of one. You can also make the fabric on a section of sock tighter by using a smaller needle size. Both of these methods throw your usual gauge calculations out the window, and only a test-knit piece will show if it affects the fit of the heel and toe.

For a lot more details about choosing just the right yarn, stitch, and construction for the toughest possible socks, check out Clara Parkes' *The Knitter's Book of Socks*.

THE START OF THE ROUND

Top-down socks are often written with the beginning of the round placed at the back of the heel, which is also the bottom of the foot. I use this convention when it suits me.

For toe-up socks, I often place the beginning of the round at the side of the sock. It runs along the edge of the toe, then up along the side of the leg. I like this because it's easier for me to keep the front and the back of the sock clearly separate in my mind. In the designs in this book, I will tell you where the beginning of the round is relative to the rest of the sock.

If you are changing colors, you may find that keeping the round on the side leads to visible jogs of color. If this bothers you, simply slip the first stitch on the second round of the new color and take special care to reduce the jog when you darn in your ends.

Short Rows and Short Row Heels

A short row is any row that doesn't use every available stitch. It may be more accurate to call them "short rounds" in socks, but we all know what we mean. Short rows are used in a lot of different sock heel turns to create shapes that otherwise wouldn't be possible. Short Row Heels and Short Row Toes are both made entirely using short rows.

Needles for Sock Knitting and Other Stuff in My Bag of Tricks

I have written all of the patterns in this book to be "needle neutral." In other words, I've described what you should do based on stitches and stitch markers, not on certain needle configurations.

You should use whatever sock needle setup makes you most comfortable, be it double-pointed needles, a 9-inch circular, two circulars, magic loop, or any other method. I've taken my

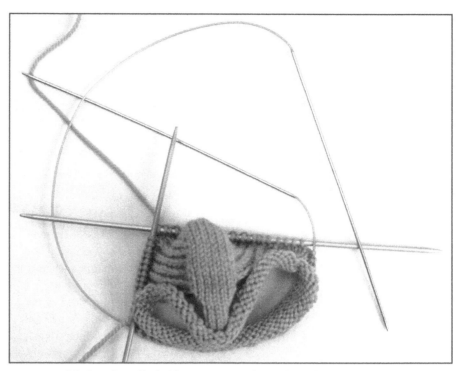

My "tiny" needle, holding instep stitches, as I work a heel flap from the toe up.

photographs with the stitches on double-pointed needles simply because those are the needles I really use.

That said, there are three pieces of specialized equipment I strongly suggest you have. The first is a good ruler. It is much easier to measure the length of feet with a ruler than with a tape measure. Also, a ruler is really the only good way to measure both gauge and the length of a sock in progress. It is so easy to deceive yourself when measuring with something that bends!

The second piece of equipment is a very small-sized circular needle with a good, flexible cable. Mine is a 16-inch US size 0 (2mm). I use it to hold instep stitches when I work a heel, to pick up dropped stitches from anywhere, and even to perform a special trick that allows me to avoid picking out waste-yarn stitches for an afterthought heel. This is the Extra Needle Technique and it has made my relationship with this heel design I love even sweeter than it was before.

Lastly, and possibly most oddly, I love having a small flashlight on hand. I alternate between the kind that goes on a keyring and the one that is built into a very cool bank-advertising pen from my grandfather, depending on which one I can find at any moment. I knit a LOT of black socks. More than once, my little light has saved my sanity while counting rows or picking up stitches.

How I Learned to Stop Worrying and Love the Graft

Grafting (also known as Kitchener stitch) isn't needed for every single type of sock. I find that grafting works very well when your sock toe ends with at least 20% of the stitches from the sock and the toe has a pretty flat shape. A round toe ends with fewer stitches and can be cinched closed like the top of a hat.

If you are going to knit top-down socks, and especially a lot of the more unusual heels in this book, your best bet is to graft.

I like to move my stitches onto lengths of dental floss before I graft. It always fits in my bag, and if I forget it, I can get it almost anywhere, unlike knitting needles. This allows me to remove the needles and really see what I'm doing, without running the risk of actually dropping stitches. Without the needles, the stitches will naturally fall into their most comfortable position, and it's easier to see which way the darning needle should go to make things work.

Now, like most knitters, I can't actually remember in what order I'm supposed to sew purl-wise and knit-wise when I graft. Instead, I just think of it as "one old, one new." After the first two stitches on any set of grafts, I simply go to the other side, take my needle through a stitch I've already been through, take it through a new stitch, and begin all over again on the other side.

Can't get over your fear of grafting, but still want to work these designs? Try the zigzag bind off or strap closure. They are both great methods, but somewhat fiddly—and, of course, look very different from a grafted section of knitting. Also, the strap closure still includes a tiny amount of grafting, but it is truly very, very small.

Dealing with Gaps

Many sock knitters have noticed that messy holes can form where the top of a heel flap meets the instep stitches. This can also happen where afterthought heels and even short-row heels meet up with the rest of the sock. Wherever some stitches are put on hold while others are worked, the stitches on hold can get stretched out. When the stitches are worked, the

extra yarn they have pulled in from their neighboring stitches can remain loose, leaving a space.

Will these floppy stitches snap back into place on their own, removing the problem? They might. If they do not, you're left with a weak spot in the knitting on a part of the sock that is already vulnerable to wear, since it can rub up against shoes.

As nature abhors a vacuum, knitters despise gaps. I have two ways to prevent gaps—and one way to cheat if they form.

1. Extra stitch(es)

Pick up one or two "extra" stitches to cover the gap, then decrease them away.

But be careful: if you pick up your "extra" stitch in between your gusset and instep stitches, you may actually create a hole that's worse than what you had before. Instead, pick up your extra stitch in line with your gusset stitches, into the meat of your sock, as it were. If you add extra stitches on one side of the gusset, don't forget to add an equal number to the other side by picking up extra stitches before you pick up the rest of them. (For more information, see the Abbreviations and Techniques section, page 129.)

2. Make a switch

For a top-down sock, on the round when you are starting the heel flap, you could switch the positions of the stitch nearest the heel flap and the first/last stitches in the heel flap.

For a toe-up sock, on the round where you are finishing the heel flap, switch the positions of the stitch nearest the heel flap and the first/last stitches in the heel flap.

For an afterthought heel, once all of the stitches for the heel have been placed onto working needles, take a

USING DENTAL FLOSS WHEN GRAFTING

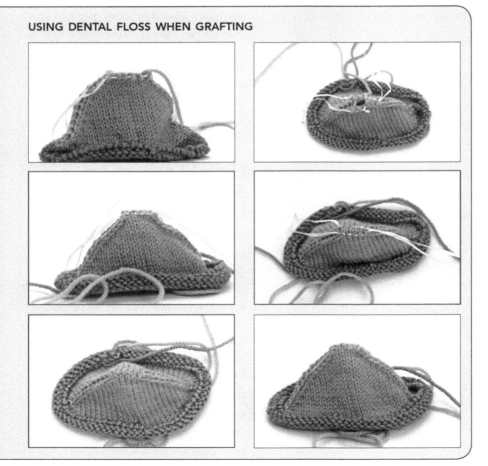

SWITCHING THE POSITIONS OF THE STITCHES NEAR THE HEEL FLAP

The left-hand photo shows the side that was switched. Note the slightly elongated stitch moving from the edge to the heel flap. The right-hand photo shows the unswitched side.

It looks pretty good, right? It looked terrible when I first made it. Sometimes the stitch smooths itself out as you are working the gusset and ignoring it.

look at the "ear" of the heel. Switch the positions of the two stitches on the edge of the ear.

Before working the first row for a short-row heel, switch the first and last stitches that will be used for the short rows with the stitches next to them.

(For more information, see the Techniques section, page 130.)

3. Darn over it.

Ignore the too-loose stitches for now, go back later with a darning needle, and duplicate-stitch that area to close the hole. This is the least-satisfactory method, in my opinion. If you don't have a loose end there, you'll have to add a length of yarn to do this, which means two extra ends to darn in. Also, you may find that the more you mess with it, the worse it gets. It's definitely not the most fun way to spend time.

A Good Cast On and the Leg

FOR A TOP-DOWN SOCK, any cast on can be used, as long as it provides sufficient stretch. Remember that the sock top must be able to fit over the heel before it even gets to the leg. This is easier to achieve with some cast-on methods than others. I prefer the long-tail cast on.

When joining to knit in the round just after the cast on, you have to be careful not to twist. This is like saying, "be careful not to over-salt the soup." Everyone has done it; we all hate it; and it may well be impossible to avoid it 100 percent of the time.

But, thankfully, there is a way to make twisting less likely. When you cast on, leave a longer tail than you normally would. Then, work the first few rows of your sock pattern back and forth, without joining. *Then* join into the round and continue as usual. This will leave a tiny seam open at the very top of your sock. Use the tail you left to close it up and hide it. It isn't a perfectly elegant solution, but it makes that first inch or so of knitting less nerve-wracking.

I like to make my sock legs with a lot of ribbing. This makes them more stretchy and keeps them from falling down. If you like stockinette stitch for your leg, that is fine; just make sure you work at least one inch of ribbing before you begin the stockinette portion. Two inches is safer.

An easy way to add shaping to a sock leg is to start with a slightly larger needle, then switch to smaller needles at some point on the leg. Make sure to take notes about when the switch is made and what both of your needle sizes are. It would be very easy to end up with a pair of socks that didn't match at all because you forgot to switch!

The length of sock legs is a matter of personal preference. As a general rule, for the standard mid-calf sock, the length of the leg should be about the same as the length of the foot. If you have measured from the floor to the desired top of the sock, be sure to reduce this measurement by about two inches to allow for the height of the heel.

Top-Down Sock Heels

FLAP-AND-GUSSET HEELS

To an extent, this sock heel closely follows the external structure of the heel of the foot. How you define and interpret that depends a little bit on what you are used to. Don't be afraid to try heels you haven't made before. You might be surprised at how easy it is to fall in love with something new.

The sock heel flap lies against the back of the foot's heel, the heel turn cups under the heel, and the gusset shaping allows the heel area of the sock to be larger around than the foot of the sock.

As the name implies, flap-and-gusset heels begin with a heel flap. The flap is worked back and forth and can be in stockinette stitch, two-yarn stockinette stitch, slipped heel stitch, Eye of Partridge, or anything else that will stand up to rubbing against the back of

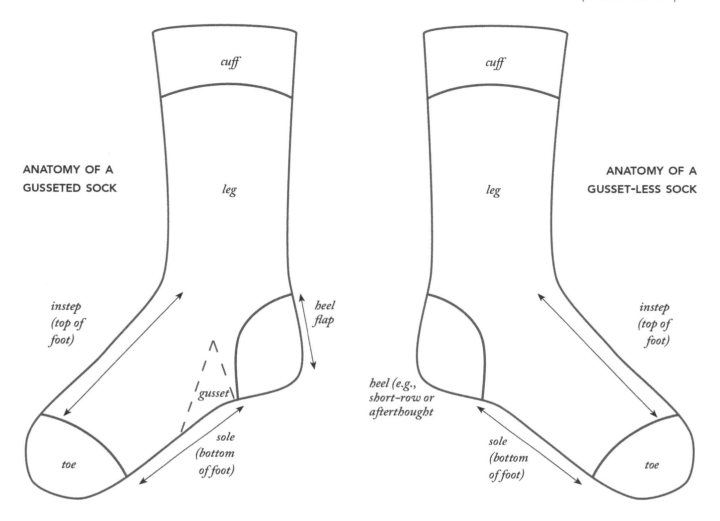

ANATOMY OF A GUSSETED SOCK

ANATOMY OF A GUSSET-LESS SOCK

TOP-DOWN HEEL TYPES AND THEIR FEATURES

	picked-up stitches	gusset	short rows	grafting	patterns in the book using this heel
Round Heel	yes	yes	yes	no	Strie, Procrastinatrix
Half-Handkerchief Heel	yes	yes	yes	no	Mouchoir
Square Heel	yes	yes	yes	no	Checked and Square
Common Heel	yes	yes	no	yes	
Shaped Common Heel	yes	yes	no	yes	Uncommon Dragon
Modified Shaped Common Heel	yes	yes	no	yes	
Balbriggan Heel	yes	sometimes	no	yes	Bootstrap
Band Heel	yes	sometimes	yes	no	Dyad
Short-Row Heel	no	no	yes	no	Arithmophobia

GAUGE: A CAUTIONARY TALE

Sometimes the relationship between stitch and row gauge is very different from the usual expectation in, say, sport-weight yarn when your stitch gauge might be 6 stitches per inch and your row gauge 8 rows per inch.

For example, I present (with horror) my first two-yarn stockinette-stitch heel flap. My gauge for the plain stockinette portion of my swatch was a relatively normal 8 sts/inch. The stitch gauge on the heel flap was more like 10½ sts/inch. This is probably a product of the two yarns being drawn tightly across the back of the stitches, and the fact that I purl as tightly as possible on heel flaps. The resulting stitch pattern resembled ribbing, really, in that the stitches stacked on top of each other.

The row gauge was 10 rows per inch, so the heel flap was over 3 inches long. This is rather enormous, since the usual heel flap length for a woman's medium sock is closer to 2½ inches. Also, 16 stitches in my "normal" stitch gauge for this sock is only 2 inches wide, so the heel flap can be a little longer than that, but not by more than 50 percent!

So, I had two choices. I could content myself with a gigantic heel flap (and find a way to pick up more than the usual 1 stitch per 2 rows for the gusset from the heel flap), or I could make a heel with fewer rows (and still find a way to pick up more than the usual 1 stitch per 2 rows for the gusset from the heel flap.)

I assumed I could maintain the same gauge a second time, and wanted a heel flap that is 2½ inches long. My row gauge was 10 rows per inch, which meant I would get 5 slipped-stitch edge chains per inch as I

worked the heel flap. In 2½ inches, I would make 12.5 chains. Let's round that to 13 (so I would need to work 26 heel-flap rows, total), and have 3 extra stitches to pick up. This is actually rather perfect, since I usually like to pick up a few extra stitches for

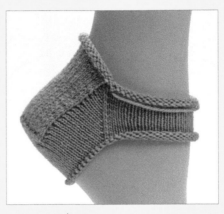

A heel flap worked over 32 sts, in two-yarn stockinette stitch (vertical stripes, one color), 32 rows long, with round heel shaping. The heel flap is way too long!

A heel flap worked over 32 sts, in two-yarn stockinette stitch (vertical stripes, two colors), 26 heel-flap rows. I picked up two extra gusset stitches at the top of the heel flap and one extra gusset stitch right next to the heel turn, on each side. This is a round heel from the top down. Much better fit!

the gusset, to take care of any floppiness at the top and bottom of the heel flap edges. I picked up two extra gusset stitches at the top of the heel flap and one extra gusset stitch right next to the heel turn, on each side.

a shoe. Reinforcing threads help with this, too, but aren't as good a solution as sturdy stitch structure.

Heel Flaps

For Balbriggan and Band Heels, jump right to those instructions now. The heel flaps for those are unique.

Most heel flaps are worked over half of the stitches used for the ankle of the sock, and most of them have as many rows as stitches, with a slipped stitch starting each row. For example, a sock that has 64 stitches at the ankle might have a heel flap that is 32 stitches wide and 32 rows long. This would leave 16 stitches that could be easily picked up through the chains on the side of the heel flap, made by slipping those stitches. (But see the next page for a cautionary tale.)

The absolute ideal length for a heel flap, according to many people, is the distance from the ankle bone of the intended wearer to the floor. In practice, I find this hard to measure accurately, but it can provide a good starting point, or at least offer a clue as to why socks aren't fitting as they should.

The moral of the story is this: you may have to fudge a bit on the number of gusset stitches to make a heel flap that fits well, because row gauge is a strange and capricious mistress. Also, it's a good idea to stop about halfway through the heel flap and measure row gauge, so that you can make adjustments, if needed.

Regardless of length, this book assumes that heel flaps should always end by working a wrong-side row, because heel-turning instructions begin on the right-side row.

STOCKINETTE STITCH

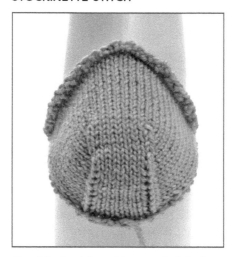

Band heel, with stockinette-stitch heel flap.

(RS): Sl1, knit to end.
(WS): Sl1, purl to end.

This stitch, possibly the most basic possible for a heel flap, has some advantages and disadvantages. It doesn't have any natural reinforcement, so it is weaker than some other options. On the other hand, it is easier to darn well if it does develop a hole.

The inherent weakness of the fabric can be mitigated by carrying a reinforcement thread along with the working yarn for the flap, adding two-stranded colorwork, or planning on showing off your socks by wearing backless shoes. The following two-yarn heel flaps use two yarns, yarn A and yarn B. You can use two ends of the same ball of yarn if you like. (Or wind off a small ball of yarn for yarn B, so that you don't drive yourself crazy untangling yarn.) The floats in the back of the work provide a tougher structure than a plain stockinette-stitch heel.

TWO-YARN STOCKINETTE STITCH (VERTICAL STRIPES)

Top-down heel flap in two-yarn stockinette stitch (vertical stripes, two colors), with a round heel.

I find that this stitch produces a heel flap that has fewer rows per inch than with other flaps, so it can sometimes be too long (see Gauge: A Cautionary Tale, page 20). Take care to measure it before you turn the heel.

Over an even number of stitches:

(RS): Sl1, [k1 with A, k1 with B] to last stitch, k1 with A.
(WS): Sl1, [p1 with B, p1 with A] to last stitch, p1 with B.

Over an odd number of stitches:

(RS): Sl1, [k1 with A, k1 with B] to end.
(WS): Sl1, [p1 with A, p1 with B] to end.

ROUND HEELS

TWO-YARN STOCKINETTE STITCH (CHECKERBOARD)

Over an even number of stitches:

(RS): Sl1, [k1 with A, k1 with B] to last stitch, k1 with A.
(WS): Sl1, [p1 with A, p1 with B] to last stitch, p1 with A.

Over an odd number of stitches:

(RS): Sl1, [k1 with A, k1 with B] to end.
(WS): Sl1, [p1 with B, p1 with A] to end.

SLIPPED HEEL STITCH

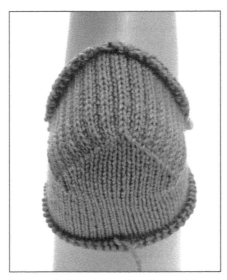

This is a half-handkerchief heel, with a slipped-stitch heel flap.

Over an even number of stitches:

(RS): [Sl1, k1] to end.
(WS): Sl1, purl to end.

Over an odd number of stitches:

(RS): [Sl1, k1] to last stitch, k1.
(WS): Sl1, purl to end.

EYE OF PARTRIDGE

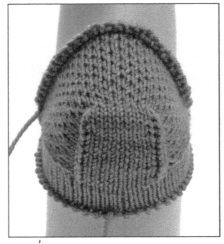

Top-down eye-of-partridge flap over 32 sts. Divided for a square heel by 11-10-11.

Over an even number of stitches:
Row 1 (RS): [Sl1, k1] to end.
Row 2 (WS): Sl1, purl to end.
Row 3 (RS): Sl1, k2, sl1, [k1, sl1] to 2 sts from end, k2.
Row 4 (WS): Sl1, purl to end.

Over an odd number of stitches:
Row 1 (RS): [Sl1, k1] to last stitch, k1.
Row 2 (WS): Sl1, purl to end.
Row 3 (RS): Sl1, k2, [sl1, k1] to end.
Row 4 (WS): Sl1, purl to end.

Extra-Long Heel Flaps

If your socks tend to crawl down into your shoe, even though you have plenty of ribbing on the leg and your sock's foot isn't too short, you may simply have a heel flap that is too short. People with long, thin feet and high arches sometimes encounter this. A bone spur on your heel might also cause this fit problem. You may have to design a heel flap that has more rows than stitches for a perfect fit. The exact percentage of extra length will be individual. Experiment to find what you need, but start with about 10 percent. For our example sock, I would round 3.2 rows up to 4 rows and try making a heel flap that is 36 rows long. You will need to pick up more than the usual number of stitches to close the gusset.

Extra-Short Heel Flaps

If your shoes are difficult to put on because your sock heel flips up and gets in the way, your heel flap might be too long. Check to make sure that your sock's foot isn't too long, as a too-long heel flap is unusual. But, if your feet are flat, or the heel of your foot is wide and short, you might need a shorter heel flap. Again, experiment and start with a small change.

How Flaps and Turns Affect Gussets

There are two factors that work together to determine exactly how many rounds are needed to complete the gusset shaping (and return to the original number of stitches for the foot). One can be changed by the knitter at will; the other is set by the type of heel turn that is used. It's not super-important to know this unless you are trying to fit in a certain number of rows (or the end of a pattern repeat) on the foot of a sock, but if you are—well, it's good to know.

Don't Be Scared, X is Just A Number

X is the number of stitches you will be working on when you begin the heel turn. It is usually half of the total stitches for the sock, and the other half will have been put on hold while you work the heel flap and heel turn.

X will be an even number or an odd number. The turns are worked in basically the same way for either one, but if X is odd, you may have to round a number up or down.

X/2, or half of these stitches, comes up a lot in heel-turn calculations, so it makes sense to make a note of it before you begin.

Heel flap length, as we have seen above, can be changed very easily. It's possible to fudge here and there by a few stitches, but you can rely on picking up about as many total stitches from the heel flap as the flap is long in rows. Half of these picked up stitches will come from one side of the heel flap and half from the other side.

Each kind of heel turn, on the other hand, will leave a unique number of stitches when it is complete. This number can only be changed if the heel shaping is altered, too.

Heel Turns

After you have worked the heel flap, it is time to turn the heel. X is the number of heel-flap stitches when you begin the heel turn. S is the number of stithes through the foot and leg of your sock.

ROUND HEEL

The round or "French" heel and the Half Handkerchief heel are both extremely common methods for turning heels. The round heel is not the easiest one to work, but it does provide a very close fit for the bottom and back of the wearer's heel on most people. Unfortunately, it is also the reason, I suspect, that many people think turning sock heels is as much witchcraft as science.

Since this is the default heel for many knitters, I will discuss the other heel turnings with this one in mind. It is really not difficult at all after you have done it about 100 times, but I hope these instructions demystify it a bit. In reality, the round heel is just a combination of short rows and decreases, and it makes a blunted little triangle connecting the heel flap to the bottom of the foot.

If X is an even number:
Row 1 (RS): Sl1, k(X/2) sts, k1, ssk, k1. Turn.
Row 2 (WS): Sl1, p5, p2tog, p1. Turn.
Row 3: Sl1, k6, ssk, k1. Turn.

Row 4: Sl1, p7, p2tog, p1. Turn.

Skip to "For both."

If X is an odd number, round X/2 down to the nearest whole number and work:

Row 1 (RS): Sl1, k(X/2) sts, k2, ssk, k1. Turn.
Row 2 (WS): Sl1, p6, p2tog, p1. Turn.
Row 3: Sl1, k7, ssk, k1. Turn.
Row 4: Sl1, p8, p2tog, p1. Turn.

For both:
Continue, working one more stitch before the decrease on each row, until you have worked all of the heel stitches. You may have to skip the final k1 and p1 on the last two rows, if you run out of stitches. Knit to the middle of the row and pm for the start of the round. Move on to picking up stitches for the gusset.

Tip: The turn on any row produces a small gap between the last stitch worked and the first stitch left unworked. The decrease is always worked using the stitches on either side of the gap. If you lose your place while working, looking for the gap can help you find your place.

The four charts on page 22 show a round heel worked over different numbers of stitches: 24, 32, 36, and 40.

With this heel, if the heel flap is X rows long, the rows to work the turn + rows to complete the gusset shaping (and return to the original number of sts) = number of stitches on the heel flap. The gusset needed is usually between S/3 and S/3.5.

SQUARE HEEL

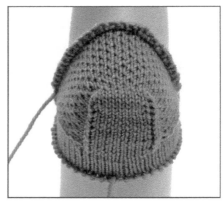

Top-down eye-of-partridge flap over 32 sts. Divided for a square heel by 11-10-11.

This heel is very easy to turn. It takes more rows to work than a round heel and creates a smaller gusset. One could argue that the deeper heel makes up for the smaller gusset. In my mind, it certainly does. Instead of staggered short rows that create a triangle as for the round heel, short rows that are all the same length make a tiny square to connect the heel flap to the bottom of the foot. I call this square the "strap" of the heel.

The instructions given below are for stockinette stitch, but you can continue whatever stitch pattern you had on the heel through this section. Just remember that the wearer will be standing on this portion of the sock, so stockinette stitch is usually a good choice.

Sometimes the very back portion of this heel can look baggy. This usually evens out with wear. If you don't like the extra fabric there, you can add some slipped stitches to the first few right-side rows to tighten it up.

Take X and divide it by 3. This will rarely be even. The goal is to make the two outside edges with the same number of stitches, and let the center of the heel fall where it may. For our example socks, our heel flap is 32 stitches wide, so I would divide it as 11, 10, 11. The central stitches will form the strap running from the back of the heel to the bottom of the foot. You can adjust the size of the strap to your taste.

If you do adjust the width of the strap, you will have to change the length, too, so take that into consideration. A wider strap makes a heel that takes fewer rows to work and will leave more stitches after the heel turn. If your gusset is shaped by decreasing by 2 sts every other round, this will produce a sock with gusset shaping that takes more rows to work than most. A more narrow strap will create the opposite situation. It will take more rows to work and leave fewer stitches available for gusset decreases. These decreases will start farther down the foot, so a smaller gusset isn't necessarily a problem.

(RS): Sl1, knit the central strap sts, ssk. Turn.
(WS): Sl1, purl the central strap sts, p2tog. Turn.

Work these 2 rows until all heel sts have been worked, stopping after a WS row. Knit to the middle of the stitches that remain, pm for the start of the round, and move on to picking up sts for the gusset.

HALF HANDKERCHIEF HEEL

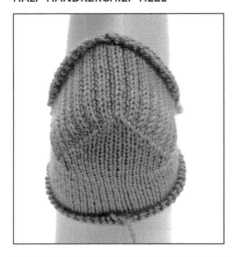

This heel is almost identical to the round heel, only the triangle has a sharper point at the very back of the heel. It also takes more rows to work the heel turn, and therefore leaves fewer stitches. Compared to a round heel worked with the same length of heel flap and the same number of gusset stitches, the heel turn will be deeper, but the gusset will be a bit narrower. This allows the actual heel of the sock to stick out a little more.

The heel-turn-to-gusset relationship is also easier to determine. In most cases, the number of rows to work the heel turn is the same as the number of stitches left when the turn is complete—and they are both roughly half of X.

The name seems to come from the triangle formed by the heel turn. In *The Ladies' Work-Table Book*, a baby's shawl is described as possible to make in either a square or "half-handkerchief" shape (Anon., p. 129). It's fair to say that "half-handkerchief" meant "triangle."

The gusset needed is around S/4.

If X is an even number:
Row 1 (RS): Sl1, k([X/2] – 1) sts, ssk, k1. Turn.
Row 2 (WS): Sl1, p1, p2tog, p1. Turn.
Row 3: Sl1, k2, ssk, k1. Turn.
Row 4: Sl1, p3, p2tog, p1. Turn.

If X is an odd number, round X/2 down to the nearest whole number and work:
Row 1 (RS): Sl1, k(X/2) sts, k1, ssk, k1. Turn.
Row 2 (WS): Sl1, p2, p2tog, p1. Turn.
Row 3: Sl1, k3, ssk, k1. Turn.
Row 4: Sl1, p4, p2tog, p1. Turn.

For both:
Continue, working one more stitch before the decrease on each row, until you have worked all of the heel stitches. For the last row, there will be no p1 after the p2tog. (Depending on the number of stitches in the heel flap, you may have to skip the last final k1 and p1 on the last two rows, if you run out of stitches.) Knit to the middle of the row and pm for the start of the round. Move on to picking up stitches for the gusset.

See the tip on "Round Heel" about what to do if you get lost.

COMMON HEEL

This heel is beyond easy and has no short rows at all, but can produce an extra, very square pocket of fabric at the back and bottom of the heel. I leave it to the knitter to decide if this looks charming or ridiculous.

You have to use grafting to finish this heel, but it's a pretty good place to practice grafting before you get to the toe.

The flap for this heel is usually some form of stockinette stitch. After your usual heel flap, add 25 percent more heel flap rows than you would for a

round heel. My usual heel flap is 2½ inches long. 1.25 × 2.5 = 3.125, or just over 3 inches. For this example heel, I worked 32 rows for a 3-inch-long flap. Work one more RS row and work a WS row until you are halfway across the row.

Finish: Break the yarn, leaving yourself a long tail. Fold the work so that the wrong sides of the heel flap are together. Using a darning needle, graft the heel flap stitches together. (If you have an odd number of heel stitches, work a k2tog before you begin grafting.)

Rejoin yarn at the center of the heel and pick up stitches for the gusset.

You may be tempted to use the tail you might have left from grafting to pick up some stitches, then join new yarn. I don't like to do this because I find that the area right at the end of the join has a tendency to look messy. So, I like to have that little tail to darn in and help firm up that area.

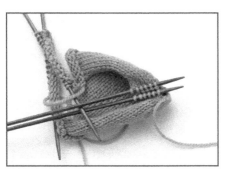

Common heel, ready to graft closed, and mid-graft.

I picked up 24 stitches from 16 slipped edges (3 stitches picked up from every 2 slipped edges), and ended up with 80 stitches before the gusset decreases.

Common heel, top-down, checkerboard two-color stockinette. Worked 32 rows for a 3"-long flap, picked up 24 sts from 16 slipped edges (3 pu from every 2 slipped edges). Ended up with 80 sts for gusset.

SHAPED COMMON HEEL

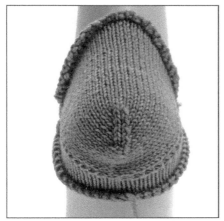

Shaped common heel, heel flap with a narrow strip of garter stitch on each side.

The Shaped Common Heel skips short rows in favor of grafting and mostly avoids the little elf hat on the back of the Common Heel. I think it is quite lovely.

The flap for this heel is usually worked in some form of stockinette stitch. I added a very small garter-stitch border to the heel flap of the sample. I love the way this looks and it makes heel-flap rows very easy to count. To follow my example yourself, work the heel flap as:

(RS): Sl1, knit to end.
(WS): Sl1, k2, purl to 3 sts from end, k3.

For a plain stockinette heel flap, work:
(RS): Sl1, knit to end.
(WS): Sl1, purl to end.

Work the "usual" number of rows for heel flap, then:

If X is an even number:
Pm at X/2 heel stitches.
(RS): Sl1, knit to 2 sts before marker, k2tog, ssk, knit to end.
(WS): Sl1, purl to end.

Rep these 2 rows until you have added 25 percent to the length of the heel flap. Work 1 more RS row and work the WS row to the marker. Finish as for the Common Heel.

If X is an odd number:
Find the stitch that is dead center and pm in front of it.
(RS): Sl1, knit to 2 sts before marker, k2tog, k1, ssk, knit to end.
(WS): Sl1, purl to end.

Rep these 2 rows until you have added 25 percent to the length of the heel flap (round down, if you need to). Work 1 more RS row. Turn; sl1, purl to 2 sts before the marker, p2tog. Finish as for the Common Heel.

MODIFIED SHAPED COMMON HEEL

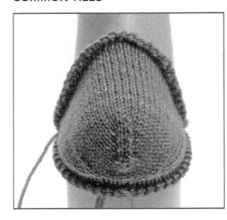

I love the Shaped Common Heel, but I wanted to make a version that is a bit shallower and has a very small gusset (it might even have no gusset at all, if your row gauge works out a certain way). So, I borrowed a cue from the Balbriggan Heel and added some decreases to shape the back of the heel.

This heel might be too shallow for people with high arches or heels that stick out a lot. But it makes a great heel for people who want less fabric there, especially children and people with square-toed feet.

(RS): Sl1, knit to end.
(WS): Sl1, purl to end.

Work these 2 rows for the heel flap until it is X × 0.8 rows long, rounding to the nearest even number. Now calculate Y:

Y = S/5, rounded down to the nearest whole number. For the example heel, I worked over 32 sts for 26 rows, then took Y as 6.

If X is an even number:
Place markers:

- 1st marker: Y sts from the beginning of the row
- 2nd marker: X/2 sts from the beginning of the row
- 3rd marker: Y sts from the end of the row

(RS): Sl1, knit to 2 sts before 1st marker, k2tog, sm, knit to 2 sts before 2nd marker, k2tog, sm, ssk, knit to 3rd marker, sm, ssk, knit to end. 4 sts decreased.
(WS): Sl1, purl to end.

Rep these 2 rows until you have 4 or 5 sts between your 1st and 2nd marker or you run out of sts before your first marker, stopping with a RS row. Work a WS row to the second marker. Finish as for the Common Heel.

If X is an odd number, round X/2 down to the nearest whole number.

Place markers:
- 1st marker: Y sts from the beginning of the row
- 2nd marker: X/2 sts from the beginning of the row
- 3rd marker: Y sts from the end of the row

(RS): Sl1, knit to 2 sts before 1st marker, k2tog, sm, knit to 2 sts before 2nd marker, k2tog, sm, k1, ssk, knit to 3rd marker, sm, ssk, knit to end. 4 sts decreased.
(WS): Sl1, purl to end.

Rep these 2 rows until you have 4 or 5 sts between your 1st and 2nd marker or you run out of sts before your first marker, stopping with a RS row. Work a WS row to the second marker. Finish as for the Common Heel.

BALBRIGGAN HEEL

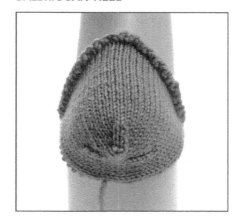

Why is it called a "Balbriggan" heel? Balbriggan is a coastal village in Ireland, north of Dublin. It was the site of Smith's Stocking Mill in the nineteenth century, which, according to visitbalbriggan.com, "made stockings for Queen Victoria, as well as men's 'Long-Johns' called Balbriggans!"

The term "Balbriggan" shows up in American newspaper advertisements for stockings and long underwear as early as 1880, but it's impossible to know if they had this kind of heel or were just associating themselves with the Balbriggan brand.

The heel is shown in *Weldon's Practical Stocking Knitter* in 1885. It is possible that the mill invented this variation on the Common Heel, and the name stuck. I think it is absolutely stunning, fun to knit and worth trying out. I have no idea why it is not as widely known as the French heel.

This is a lovely but rather shallow heel that traditionally ends up with a very small (or no) gusset. If you like the look

of it but want a deeper heel and a more generous gusset, simply work more rows before you add the markers.

The difference between the Balbriggan Heel and the Shaped Common Heel lies in the way the decreases are worked. Work as for the Shaped Common Heel until you have placed your markers.

(RS): Sl1, knit to 1st marker, sm, ssk, knit to 2 sts before 2nd marker, k2tog, sm, ssk, knit to 2 sts before 3rd marker, k2tog, sm, knit to end. 4 sts decreased.
(WS): Sl1, purl to end.

Rep these 2 rows until you have 4 sts between your first and second marker. Work 1 more RS row and work the WS row to the 2nd marker. Finish as for the Common Heel.

If X is an odd number:
Round X/2 down to the nearest whole number; place markers at Y sts from the beginning of the row, X/2 sts, and Y sts from the end of the row.

(RS): Sl1, knit to 1st marker, sm, ssk, knit to 2 sts before 2nd marker, k2tog, sm, k1, ssk, knit to 2 sts before 3rd marker, k2tog, sm, knit to end. 4 sts decreased.
(WS): Sl1, purl to end.

Rep these 2 rows until you have 4 or 5 sts between your first and second marker. Work 1 more RS row and work the WS row to the second marker. Finish as for the Common Heel.

BAND HEEL

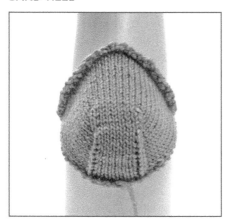

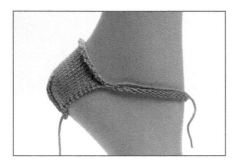

This is not the best heel for a sock when S is smaller than 32.

With this heel your gusset shaping is worked as you are turning the heel. You will be able to just knit straight on for the foot after picking up the gusset stitches. It hugs the foot very well. If you are worried that the area around the instep join will be too tight for the wearer, I strongly suggest a test-knit piece that goes from the top of the heel flap through the gusset, and about an inch of foot after that. Put the test piece on a piece of waste yarn or very flexible circular needle and try it on.

The heel is worked in three parts:

Part 1
(RS): Sl1, knit to end.
(WS): Sl1, purl to end.

Work these 2 rows for the heel flap until it is X × 0.6 rows long, rounding to the nearest even number. (In our example of a 32-stitch heel flap, you would work 20 rows in part 1.)

Part 2

This gets a little crazy, but stay with me. Let's say (X/4) − 2 is R. (X − R)/2 is the number of stitches we want to mark off at the beginning and end of this first row. If you mess around with algebra, you'll see that this number comes out to 1 + (3X/8).

To put it another, less frightening way, you need to figure out (X/4) − 2 and mark those off as your center stitches.

X/4 is the number of stitches you will have left over after shaping is finished. If X is odd, this needs to be odd. If X is even, this needs to be even.

(So, for example, X/4 is 8, X/4 − 2 is 6, [X − (X/4 − 2)]/2 is 13, so at this point you end up with 13 sts, 1st marker, 6 sts, 2nd marker, followed by 13 more sts.)

(RS): Sl1, knit to 2 sts from 1st marker, k2tog, sm, knit to 2nd marker, sm, ssk, knit to end of row. (2 sts decreased.)
(WS): Sl1, purl to end of row.

Rep these 2 rows X/10 times, rounding down to the nearest whole number. In our example sock, we would rep those rows 3 times.

Part 3

(RS): Sl1, knit to 2nd marker, sm, ssk. Turn.
(WS): Sl1, purl to 1st marker, sm, p2tog. Turn.

Work these 2 rows until you have X/4 stitches left, stopping after a WS row. Knit to middle of the stitches that remain, pm for the start of the round, and move on to picking up stitches for the foot. For our example, we take the 8 stitches left over, knit 4 of them, pm, and move on to picking up.

Check the math on your total heel flap rows before you begin, to make sure you don't need to adjust the number of rows before you begin part 3. In our example, we worked 26 rows of heel flap, total (only parts 1 and 2 contribute to this number), and had 8 stitches left

over. 26 + 8 = 34. So, we could either work one pair of gusset decreases or work 2 fewer rows in part 1.

The Gusset

Once the heel has been turned, stitches must be picked up to close the sock and continue on the foot. There are usually extra stitches that need to be decreased away until the sock foot is the same width as the sock ankle. Those stitches form a small triangle on either side of the foot and are called the gusset.

PICKING UP GUSSET STITCHES

Pick up and knit stitches through each slipped-stitch edge of the heel flap. If this method causes gaps to form that bother you, take a look at "Dealing with Gaps" on page 16.

1. As in the photos above, you could pick up an extra stitch or two there, while you are picking up

PLACING GUSSET DECREASES

Some knitting patterns will place the line of gusset decreases right next to the instep stitches, and some will put them one stitch lower. This moves the stress of the line of decreases (and the possible small gap they could cause) away from the intersection of the instep and the picked-up gusset stitches.

If you want to see how it works, simply mentally (or physically) move one stitch from the stitches you picked up on either side of the gusset so that they are with the instep stitches.

gusset stitches, and simply decrease them away along with the gusset stitches.

2. On the round when you are starting the heel flap (see below), you could switch the positions of the stitch nearest the heel flap and the first/last stitches in the heel flap.

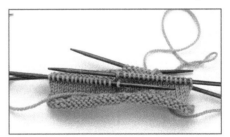

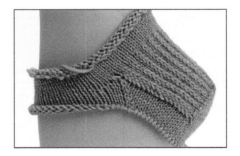

This is the side that was switched. Note the slightly elongated stitch moving from the edge to the heel flap.

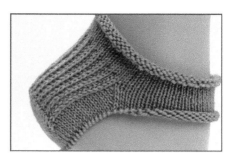

This is the unswitched side. It looks pretty good, right? It looked terrible when I first made it. Sometimes the stitch smooths itself out as you are working the gusset and ignoring it.

3. Ignore the too-loose stitches for now, go back later with a darning needle, and duplicate-stitch that area to close the hole.

DECREASING GUSSET STITCHES

Most instructions for flap-and-gusset heels place the beginning of the round for the sock at the center of the heel stitches after the heel is turned. I've kept these instructions in line with that tradition for this type of heel. Gussets can be shaped in a variety of ways, but the following method is the most common.

Along with a stitch marker for the beginning of the round, I also like to pm on either side of my gusset stitches. For example, I would have a marker for the beginning of the round, knit across half of the heel stitches, pick up stitches for the right side of the gusset, pm, knit across the instep, pm, pick up stitches for the left side of the gusset, knit to end of round. You could also arrange the stitches on your needles so that the gusset decreases fall on the ends of your needles.

Rnd 1: Knit to 2 sts before the marker, k2tog, knit to marker, ssk, knit to end of rnd.
Rnd 2: Knit.

These two rounds are repeated until the sock has the same number of stitches as it had at the ankle. If your ankle and ball of foot measurements are very different, you can customize your sock by having more or fewer stitches after the gusset decreases.

AFTERTHOUGHT HEELS WITH GUSSETS

Afterthought heels, also called inserted heels, are great for when you just don't want to work a heel along with the sock—like when you're knitting in the dark or on a plane and are getting motion-sick anyway. I also like them because they open up a lot of style and construction possibilities that might otherwise be hard to work. Additionally, if you are really unsure about the amount of yarn you have, you can make an afterthought heel in another color.

As an extra bonus, if your heel ever wears out, it is relatively easy to remove and replace it.

And finally, who doesn't want to be asked, over and over again, what the heck they might be knitting? Leaving the heel off a sock certainly gets you more attention from the non-knitting public.

You need to know how many stitches will be left on the heel after the heel is turned. (This is the same number of stitches as would be added to your original number of stitches after you pick up the gusset stitches.) If you need to estimate, round up. Too many gusset stitches is better than too few. Each heel turn in this book includes details on calculating the gusset stitches needed for it.

Using a provisional cast on (see page 130), add half of the gusset stitches, knit across the heel flap stitches using waste yarn, add the other half of the gusset stitches (with a provisional cast on), then return to your working yarn, work across the new stitches, and work the rest of the round. If you plan well, you can use the same waste yarn for knitting and casting on.

Treat these cast-on gusset stitches exactly like regular gusset stitches. Decrease them away on every other round on the foot until they are gone.

You will have to figure out how many rows will be added by the heel turn. For a round heel, this is the number of heel-flap stitches minus the gusset stitches.

As an example, let's consider a 64-stitch sock, worked from the top down. After the leg is complete on such a sock, I would drop the working yarn. With waste yarn, I cast on 9 stitches, knit 32 stitches with waste yarn, and cast on 9 more stitches. Returning to my working yarn, I would knit across all of the stitches I just made or worked with waste yarn. I would then decrease away 18 stitches in the next 18 rounds in the usual way, returning me to my original 64 stitches.

The heel turn, when I make it, would take $32 - 18 = 14$ rows to work. So, I begin the toe shaping when the whole foot is 14 rows shorter than usual, measuring from where I have left my tiny needle.

When you are otherwise finished with the sock, remove the waste yarn. Then, slide the heel-flap stitches onto the working needles and create the flap-and-gusset heel you desire, using decreases at either edge of the heel flap (ssk on the RS and p2tog on the WS) to close it to the gusset stitches. After you have turned the heel, graft the heel stitches to the remaining stitches on the bottom of the sock. (For photos of this process, see page 30).

Extra Needle Technique

Instead of leaving your afterthought heel stitches waiting on waste yarn, you can instead use an extra needle or two to hold your stitches. I have had the most success using one very flexible, very skinny circular knitting needle.

**THE GUSSETED
AFTERTHOUGHT HEEL,
STEP BY STEP**

Work across the stitches you are going to leave behind. Slip those stitches onto your tiny needle. Pull an 8-inch loop of working yarn out. This loop serves two purposes. It gives you something to tension against as you work. Later, it will be cut and the ends used to close any gaps. I tried working this without the loop, and I just couldn't get the tension to be consistent.

Anchor the top of this loop however you see fit. I sometimes end up holding it in my teeth, but if you are less strange, I suppose you could loop it around your left wrist or hold it on your left pinkie finger. In any case, you need a little bit of tension on it, at least at first, to keep things from getting too messy. It doesn't hurt anything if this loop is super-long.

Draw the tiny needle through the stitches and turn the needle point so that it faces to your right. Hold an empty working needle along the top of it. Bring the working yarn, from the back to the front, in between the two needles. This is the starting position for casting on new stitches by wrapping the working yarn around the needles.

Wrap your working yarn around both needles, away from you below the needles, and toward you above the needles, as many times as needed to replace the stitches you just left on one end of the tiny needle, plus all of the gusset stitches you need. When finished, bring the yarn, one more time, away from you below the needles, then from the back to the front, in between the two needles.

Slide the newly made stitches down to the flexible part of the circular needle, to release the tension on the wraps. Work across your working needle. This procedure will have broken the round of your sock. When you reach the end of this row, make sure your stitches aren't twisted, and join to work in the round again.

Continue on your way, leaving the tiny needle alone. If the cord on your needle is flexible enough, you should have no trouble. If you find this difficult, or you don't have a needle that is that forgiving, you could use two different needles for this technique, one for your old stitches and one for your new ones, but I really do recommend a flexible needle for the cast-on section.

When you are all finished and ready to work the heel, you should be able to join on new yarn and simply work from there. Any heel with a flap and gusset can be made, either from the top down or the toe up, no matter which way the sock was worked. After it is all finished, cut the big loop you made in half and use the two ends to neaten up the junction.

This video shows the technique: <vimeo.com/61307799> For a toe-up sock, the procedure is almost the same. You don't need to cast on gusset stitches, since you will have added them before getting ready to add the Extra Needle. Simply leave the gusset and heel-flap stitches on hold on the Extra Needle and cast on X sts to continue onto the back of the leg.

AFTERTHOUGHT HEELS WITHOUT GUSSETS

There is more than one way to prepare your sock for this kind of heel. Here are a few of them.

Planned Heel, Yarn Technique

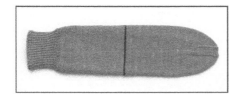

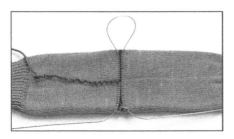

When you reach the point in the sock where you want your heel to go, work half of your stitches with waste yarn, then work them again with your working yarn. This leaves a single row of different yarn, for half of your sock's circumference. When ready, simply pull out the waste yarn and place stitches on needles. For extra security, I sometimes use my tiny needle to pick up stitches before I remove the waste yarn.

Fearless Jedi Heel

Make your sock with abandon, working away and ignoring the heel. When you are finished, determine where you want the heel to go and cut a stitch in the center of what would be the half-round for your heel. Pull back stitches until the heel stitches are free and go from there.

Extra Needle Technique

Please see my earlier notes on this technique (page 29). They apply in exactly the same way, without the gusset stitches.

WORKING A STRAP CLOSURE ON A THUMB-JOINT FLAT TOP HEEL

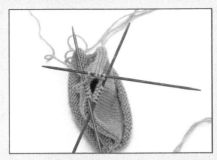

Closing Pesky Gaps

A problem some knitters have with afterthought heels is holes at the corners, where the yarn of the stitches left on hold leaps from one side of the sock to the other. One way to handle this is to pick up two or three stitches to cover the gap, then decrease them away.

If you pick up those extra stitches at least one full stitch into the meat of the knitting, your gaps will disappear. Cat Bordhi showed me this. She is totally awesome. She covers a different construction method for snipping and making sure your stitches are secure in her Houdini Socks pattern <ravelry.com/patterns/library/houdini-socks>.

Take S as your total number of stitches on needles, before you begin decreases. In this case, S is the total number of stitches that will be worked for the heel. There is no flap, so no dividing in half to get to X.

THUMB-JOINT HAT TOP HEEL/TOE

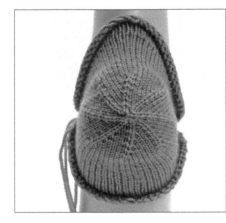

This is a round, blunt toe shape.

Knit all stitches until the heel is as deep as the distance between the tip of the intended wearer's thumb and the first joint in the thumb (mine is about 1¼ inches). As a general rule, Priscilla Gibson-Roberts in *Ethnic Socks & Stockings: A Compendium of Eastern Design and Technique* suggests using 10–15 percent of the distance from toe to ankle if you can't measure the wearer's thumb directly.

This heel can also be worked as a toe. It takes $[(S - 16)/4] + 2$ rounds to complete, once the decreases begin.

Begin decreases:
Rnd 1: Knit.
Rnd 2: [K([S/8] − 2), k2tog] around. 8 sts decreased.

Continue until $[(S/8) − 2] = 0$ (16 sts total), work Rnd 1 once more, then k2tog around twice (4 sts total). Break yarn, draw through stitches to secure.

Katherine Misegades told me the 2½-inch rule. You should check out her book *...And a Time to Knit Stockings*, available on CD from Schoolhouse Press.

THUMB-JOINT FLAT TOP HEEL/TOE

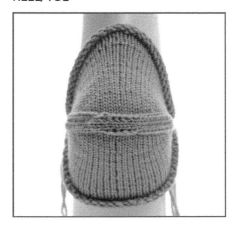

The flat-top toe looks way too wide on the fake foot, but fits a wide or square foot very well.

As for the previous heel, knit all stitches until the heel is as deep as the distance between the tip of the intended wearer's thumb and the first joint in the thumb (mine is about 1¼"). Again, as a general rule, Priscilla Gibson-Roberts suggests using 10–15 percent of the distance from toe to ankle if you can't measure the wearer's thumb directly.

This heel can also be worked as a somewhat blunt toe, and looks pretty darn cool, in my opinion.

Begin decreases:
Pm at the beginning of the rnd and at S/2 around.

Every round is the same: [K1, ssk, knit to 3 sts before marker, k2tog, k1, sm] twice. 4 sts decreased.

Continue until the heel is 2½" deep or you have 0.33 of the original stitches left. (For example, if you start with 72 sts, you might want to stop with 24 sts.) Graft the front half and the back half of the heel together (or use the strap closure on page 33).

90-DEGREE HEEL/TOE

This makes a lovely, somewhat pointed toe.

Up to a point, you can make this heel/toe more or less deep, according to your taste.

Pm at the beginning of the rnd and at S/2 around.

Rnd 1: Knit.

Rnd 2: (K1, ssk, knit to 3 sts before marker, k2tog, k1, sm) twice for a rnd. 4 sts decreased.

Continue until the heel is 2½" deep or you have 0.33 of the original stitches left. (For example, if you start with 72 sts, you might want to stop with 24 sts.) Graft the front half and the back half of the heel together (or use the strap closure, see below).

STRAP CLOSURE (OVER 4 STS)

Start with K1, ssk. Turn.
Row 1: Sl1, p2, p2tog. Turn.
Row 2: Sl1, k2, ssk. Turn.

Repeat these 2 (very short) rows until 8 stitches remain. Graft the working stitches and the other 4 stitches together. The strap closure can be as narrow or wide as you like, although I'm not sure how one would make it smaller than 2 stitches across.

SHORT-ROW HEEL/TOE

This makes a heel that fits a lot like a machine-made sock. It's a good first-sock technique, because you can use the same method for both the heel and the toe of your socks. There are no gusset stitches. For a real in-depth look at short-row heels and toes, get a copy of Priscilla Gibson-Roberts' *Simple Socks Plain and Fancy.* It's a wonderful book and really explores the design potential inherent in this easy-to-knit style.

There are many ways to work a short-row heel/toe. My favorite uses increases on the shorter short rows and decreases on the longer short rows. (I know, it seems kind of backwards, but stay with me.) Start by arranging your stitches so that your non-heel stitches are on hold and your heel stitches are ready to work.

A lot of knitters will be familiar with a wrap-and-turn method of working short rows. It works very well, but I always end up with floppy stitches when I work them. Also, I find picking

I used a short row toe and heel for my Arithmophobia Socks.

up the wraps to be impossible with black socks. So, I prefer to use decreases to prevent gaps.

Many people work short-row heels over half of their sock's stitches. However, this isn't set in stone. In her *Knitter's Book of Socks*, Clara Parkes writes that "Lucy Neatby advises that you use 60 percent of your total stitches for short-row heels."[*] This makes the heel deeper, overall, and might make it wear better.

These instructions work for narrow, medium, and wide short-row heels and toes. The only change for each one is

---

when the shorter short rows become the longer short rows, and how many stitches are involved at the turn.

Shorter Short Row 1 (RS): Sl1, k(X – 1), m1L. Turn.

Shorter Short Row 2 (WS): Sl1, p(X – 2), m1P. Turn. Continue, working 1 fewer stitch on each row before making your increase.

For a narrow heel/toe: Work until you work a row where you purl only about X/3 sts. You will have worked around 2X/3 rows, but, in this case, the number of stitches worked matters more. Make sure you stop after working a WS row.

For a medium heel/toe: Work until you work a row that uses only X/2 sts. You will have worked X/2 rows. Even if X is odd, make sure you stop after working a WS row.

For a wide heel/toe: Work until you work a row where you purl only around 2X/3 sts. You will have worked about X/3 rows, but in this case, the number of stitches worked matters more. Make sure you stop after working a WS row. At some gauges, this heel/toe will be extremely short. It might work great for a toe, but it may really be too shallow for a heel. You might want to choose a medium or narrow heel, instead.

Last Shorter Short Row for narrow heel/toe (WS): Sl1, p(X/3), m1P. Turn.

Turning Row 1 (RS): Sl1, k[(X/3) – 1], ssk, k1. Turn.
Turning Row 2 (WS): Sl1, p[(X/3) – 1], p2tog, p1. Turn.

Longer Short Row 1 (RS): Sl1, k(X/3), ssk, k1. Turn.
Longer Short Row 2 (WS): Sl1, k(X/3 +1), ssk, k1. Turn.

Last Shorter Short Row for medium heel/toe (WS): Sl1, p(X/2), m1P. Turn.

Turning Row 1 (RS): Sl1, k[(X/2) – 1], ssk, k1. Turn.
Turning Row 2 (WS): Sl1, p[(X/2) – 1], p2tog, p1. Turn.

Longer Short Row 1 (RS): Sl1, k(X/2), ssk, k1. Turn.
Longer Short Row 2 (WS): Sl1, p(X/2 + 1), p2tog, p1. Turn.

Last Shorter Short Row for wide heel/ toe (WS): Sl1, p(2X/3), m1P. Turn.

Turning Row 1 (RS): Sl1, k[(2X/3) – 1], ssk, k1. Turn.
Turning Row 2 (WS): Sl1, [(2X/3) – 1], p2tog, p1. Turn.

Longer Short Row 1 (RS): Sl1, k(2X/3), ssk, k1. Turn.
Longer Short Row 2 (WS): Sl1, p[(2X/3) + 1], p2tog, p1. Turn.

Continue, working 1 more stitch on each row before making your decrease, until you work a row that uses all of your heel stitches. In some circumstances, your heel will end up being more stable if you work an extra longer row or two, and use a few stitches that weren't part of the original heel.

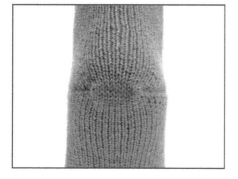

CHECK FOR FOURS

Wherever I have written, for example, *Repeat Rounds 1 and 2 until you have 0.6 × S stitches on the needles. Repeat only Round 1 until you have 0.3 × S stitches on the needles.* I should have said, *Repeat Rounds 1 and 2 until you have approximately 0.6 × S stitches on the needles. Repeat only Round 1 until you have approximately 0.3 × S stitches on the needles.*

This is precisely the kind of thing that leads knitters to pay designers (and designers to worship technical editors) to figure out the math for them. You see, 0.6 × S, 0.3 × S and S don't always play well together. But, for the toe to work, they have to! Even worse, they have to manage to be multiples of four away from each other, or the math doesn't work. That's because our decrease rounds on this type of toe always take away four stitches. (For a toe-up sock, increase rounds will always add four stitches.)

So, when I'm working out a toe, I jot down my basic math first, then I do what I call "checking for fours." For multiple sizes, you really must have a spreadsheet, but I'll try to lay it out on example clearly here.

This is for a short wedge toe on a 64-stitch sock.

S = 64

$0.6 × S = 38.4$
$0.3 × S = 19.2$

$(0.6 × S)$ rounded, just to make it whole = 38
$(0.3 × S)$ rounded, just to make it whole = 20

First, check to see if that first series of decreases could result in 38.

$64 − 38 = 26$

26 isn't a multiple of 4, but 28 is, so let's say we switch to the higher rate of decreases when we have $64 − 28 = 36$ stitches.

The last series of decreases would then go from 36 to about 20 stitches.

$36 − 20 = 16$ (which does work!)

You can also take this chance to calculate *exactly* how many rounds are needed to make this toe, with *your* numbers. $28 / 4 = 7$, so the first sets of decreases need 14 rows to work. The last 16 stitches will be decreased in just 4 rounds. This entire toe will take just $14 + 4 = 18$ rounds to work. (Our general estimate, which I got from doing a lot of algebra, estimates 17.6 rounds for this toe.)

You need the same kinds of estimates and checks when designing a toe-up sock toe. Most often, a change of just 2 or 4 stitches at the cast-on can make a big difference in how well the math for the toe comes out, so it's always worth it to spend a few minutes with a pencil and paper before casting on.

It would be cheating to do S = 64 again, so let's look at S = 68 with a medium wedge toe.

S = 68

$0.5 × S = 34$
$0.2 × S = 13.6$

$(.2 × S)$ rounded, just to make it whole = 14

$34 − 14 = 20$, which does work, so we would be OK up to the change in increase rate.

But, $68 − 34 = 34$, which isn't divisible by 4.

So, we need to make an adjustment: $68 − 36 = 32$.

$32 − 12 = 20$

This makes the cast on 12 stitches, which will be increased 5 times to 32, which will then be increased 9 times to 68. This makes the toe a total of $5 + 18 = 23$ rounds long, only a little longer than predicted by algebra (22.1).

What about the cast on or grafted round, you say? Count it, if you like, but I tend to ignore it. Something has to account for the fact that the very front of a foot isn't a perfect geometric form.

Top-Down Sock Toes

These are some of my favorite sock toes. Some knitters find that working a k2tog and an ssk right next to each other can form a bit of a gap between them. If this bothers you, try the "wide" toe described on page 39.

WEDGE TOE SETUP

Take S as your total number of stitches on the foot and place one marker 0.25 × S away from the beginning of the round and another 0.75 × S away from the beginning of the round. In our example sock, that means one marker placed 16 stitches from the beginning and another marker 48 stitches from the beginning (32 stitches from the first marker).

Rnd 1: [Knit to 2 sts before marker, k2tog, sm, ssk] twice, knit to end of rnd.
Rnd 2: Knit.

SHORT WEDGE TOE

This toe takes about 0.275 × S rnds to work.

Repeat Rounds 1 and 2 until you have 0.6 × S stitches on the needles. Repeat only Round 1 until you have 0.3 × S stitches on the needles.

Skip to "To complete all wedge toes …" on this page.

MEDIUM WEDGE TOE

This toe takes about 0.325 × S rnds to work.

Repeat Rounds 1 and 2 until you have 0.5 × S stitches on the needles. Repeat only Round 1 until you have 0.2 × S stitches on the needles.

Skip to "To complete all wedge toes …"

LONG WEDGE TOE

This toe takes about 0.45 × S rnds to work.

Rnd 1: [Knit to 2 sts before marker, k2tog, sm, ssk] twice, knit to end of rnd.
Rnds 2 and 3: Knit.

Repeat Rounds 1–3 until you have 0.5 × S stitches on the needles. Repeat only Round 1 until you have 0.2 × S stitches on the needles.

To complete all wedge toes (short, medium, or long): Knit to marker, graft remaining stitches closed.

"WIDE" TOE

This name is somewhat misleading because it doesn't refer to the shape of the toe as it lies on the foot, but rather to what the sock looks like from the side. Any of the wedge toes can be made as wide toes. Simply move the line of decreases out by one, two or three stitches, to create a wider look.

Work the instructions for the length of toe you have chosen, changing only Round 1. For example, a 4-stitch-wide "wide" toe would have this as Round 1:

Rnd 1: [Knit to 3 sts before marker, k2tog, k1, sm, k1, ssk] twice, knit to end of rnd.

SIDEWAYS TOE/HEEL

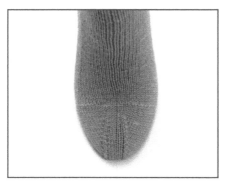

The Sideways Toe/Heel is worked like a wedge toe turned on its side.

The toe ends with approximately 0.2 × S stitches, half on the top of the toe and half on the bottom of the toe.

Calculate 0.2 × S. Round it so that it is divisible by 4. Divide it by 2. Subtract 2 from it. This is the number of stitches that will be in between your decreases as you work the toe.

For example, if S is 64, 0.2 × S is 12.8. Round that to 12. 12 divided by 2 is 6. 6 minus 2 is 4.

Rnd 1: [Knit to 4 sts before marker, k2tog, k4, ssk] twice, knit to end of rnd. Rnd 2: Knit.

Short Sideways Toe/Heel

This toe takes about 0.3 × S rnds to work.

Repeat Rounds 1 and 2 until you have 0.6 × S sts on the needles. Skip to "To complete all sideways toes/heels …"

Medium Sideways Toe/Heel

This toe takes about 0.325 × S rnds to work.

Repeat Rounds 1 and 2 until you have 0.5 × S sts on the needles. Skip to "To complete all sideways toes/heels …"

Long Sideways Toe/Heel

This toe takes about 0.45 × S rnds to work.

Rnd 1: [Knit to 2 sts before marker, k2tog, knit to marker, ssk] twice, knit to end of rnd. 4 sts decreased. Rnds 2 and 3: Knit.

Repeat Rnds 1–3 until you have 0.5 × S sts on the needles.

To complete all sideways toes/heels (short, medium, or long):
Repeat only Round 1 until you have approximately 0.2 × S sts on the needles. Graft remaining stitches closed.

Round Toe

To work this toe, the number of stitches for the foot must be divisible by 8. If it isn't, decrease stitches to a number divisible by 8 on the round before toe shaping begins.

You need as many stitch markers to make this toe as you have multiples of 8 stitches. For example, a 72-stitch sock will need 9 stitch markers.

Setup Rnd: [K8, pm] around.
Rnd 1: [Knit to 2 sts before marker, k2tog] around.

And now, a question: How many stitches did you knit on the last round between decreases? Knit that many rounds before decreasing again.

Repeat these sets of rounds until the answer to the question is "1."

Next rnd: Knit, removing markers as you go.
Next rnd: K2tog around.

If you feel there are still too many stitches to form a nice closure, work another round or two of all k2tog.

Break yarn, leaving a 6-inch tail. With a darning needle, thread the yarn through the remaining stitches. Go through twice, if you want the extra security. Pull the stitches tightly, bring the yarn to the inside of the sock and darn the tail in.

Swirl Toe

To work this toe, the number of stitches for the foot must be divisible by 4. If it isn't, decrease stitches to a number divisible by 4 on the round before toe shaping begins.

Take S as your total number of stitches on the foot and pm 0.25 × S away from the beginning of the round, another 0.5 × S away, and another 0.75 × S away. In our example sock, markers would be after stitches 16, 32, and 48 stitches from the beginning of the round.

Rnd 1: [Knit to 2 sts before marker, k2tog] around. 4 sts decreased.
Rnd 2: Knit.

Repeat these 2 rnds S/10 times, then work only Round 1 until 4 sts remain. Finish as for the Round Toe.

Short-Row Heel/Toe

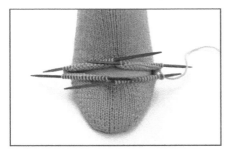

See page 33 for a thorough discussion of short-row heels and toes. The only other thing you should know is that sock toes, unlike heels, really must be started over half of the stitches, otherwise, where would they end up?

After you have finished all of your short rows, graft your working stitches to the stitches you left on hold.

Casting On

SINCE YOUR CAST ON WILL form the front of the toe, special attention is required for almost every toe-up sock toe. The exception is the short-row toe, where the cast-on edge is later picked up and worked for part of the foot.

In her book *Ethnic Socks & Stockings: A Compendium of Eastern Design and Technique*, Priscilla Gibson-Roberts defines and illustrates eight different methods for casting on at the toe end. They are all very interesting and worth further study. However, my favorite method is also the easiest one I've come across: Judy's Magic Cast On: <knitty.com/ISSUEspring06/FEATmagiccaston.html>.

You can avoid casting on, really, almost altogether if you make a rectangular toe start. Simply use a provisional cast on to make 4 stitches, then knit 1 row, purl 1 row, slipping the first stitch of every row, until you have made $(S - 8) \times 0.2$ rows. From the right side, pick up and knit 1 stitch from every slipped-stitch chain down one side of your rectangle, pick up 4 stitches from your cast on edge, pick up and knit 1 stitch from every slipped-stitch chain from the other side of your rectangle. You should now have $S \times 0.2$ stitches on your needles. From here continue shaping as for a wedge toe.

I've also written what I call the "Training Wheel" toe (see page 40). It uses a few short rows to start a Wedge toe. It looks just a tiny bit funny when it has just been made, but time and wear flattens it out.

Toe-Up Toes

My "wedge" toes have a faster rate of increase near the tip of the toe than near the body of the foot, to mimic the shape of actual toes more closely. Short toes start with more stitches and keep up the faster rate of increases longer. Long toes start with fewer stitches, make the switch to a slower rate of increase sooner, and, once there, increase at a pretty slow rate. Medium toes are right in the middle.

They all start with a certain number to be cast on, which should be an even, whole number, using Judy Magic Cast On.

(Sadly, you can't cast on just *any* number. Please see my note explaining this on page 35: Check for Fours.)

Knit 1 round, placing a marker for the beginning of the round and another one halfway around your toe.

Rnd 1: K1, m1L, knit to 1 stitch before the marker, m1R, k1, sm, k1, m1L, knit to 1 stitch before the end of the rnd, m1R, k1. 4 sts increased.
Rnds 2 and 3: Knit.

Round 1 is worked until the toe reaches a certain number of stitches. The rate of increases then slows down.

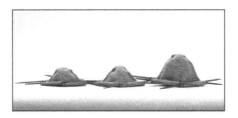

SHORT WEDGE TOE

Cast on approximately $S \times 0.3$ stitches.

Repeat Round 1 until you have approximately $S \times 0.6$ sts on the needles.

Repeat Rounds 1 and 2 until you have S sts on the needles.

MEDIUM WEDGE TOE

Cast on approximately S × 0.2 stitches.

Repeat Round 1 until you have approximately S × 0.5 sts on the needles.

Repeat Rounds 1 and 2 until you have S sts on the needles.

LONG WEDGE TOE

Cast on approximately S × 0.2 stitches.

Repeat Round 1 until you have approximately S × 0.5 sts on the needles.

Repeat Rounds 1–3 until you have S sts on the needles.

"WIDE" TOES

This name is somewhat misleading because it doesn't refer to the shape of the toe as it lies on the foot, but rather to what the sock looks like from the side. Any of the wedge toes can be made as wide toes. Simply move the line of increases out by one, two or three stitches, to create a wider look.

For example, to work a Medium "Wide" toe, take S × 0.2 stitches and round it so that it is an even number, if needed. Cast on that number of stitches, using Judy Becker's Magic Cast On. Knit one round, placing a marker for the beginning of the round and another one halfway around your toe.

Rnd 1: Knit 2, m1L, knit to 2 sts before marker, m1R, k4, m1L, knit to 2 sts before end of rnd, m1R, k2. 4 sts increased.

Repeat this round until you have approximately S × 0.5 sts on the needles.

Rnd 1: Knit 2, m1L, knit to 2 sts before marker, m1R, k4, m1L, knit to 2 sts before end of rnd, m1R, k2. 4 sts increased.
Rnd 2: Knit.

Repeat these 2 rounds until you have S sts on the needles.

SIDEWAYS TOE

This is a wide wedge toe turned on its side, and it begins in that position to make the transition from the cast-on edge as smooth as possible. These instructions are for a medium-depth toe, but it could easily be made short or long, too.

Take S × 0.2 stitches and, if necessary, round the result to an even, whole number. Cast on that number of stitches, using Judy Becker's Magic Cast On. Knit 1 round. Now, divide what you have cast on by 2. Let's call this number of stitches C.

Setup Rnd 1: K1, m1L, k(C−2), m1R, k2, m1L, k(C−2), m1R, k1. 4 sts increased.
Setup Rnd 2: K2, m1L, pm, k(C−2), pm, m1R, k4, m1L, pm, k(C−2), pm, m1R, k2. 4 sts increased.

Rnd 1: [Knit to marker, m1R, sm, knit to marker, sm, m1L] twice, knit to end. 4 sts increased.

Repeat Round 1 until you have approximately S × 0.5 sts on the needles.

Rnd 1: [Knit to marker, m1R, sm, knit to marker, sm, m1L] twice, knit to end. 4 sts increased.
Rnd 2: Knit.

Repeat these 2 rounds until you have S sts on the needles.

ROUND TOE

To work this toe, the number of stitches for the foot must be divisible by 8. Using Emily Ocker's circular beginning (see page "Emily Ocker's Circular Beginning" on page 130), leave a tail of yarn at least 4 inches long and start with S/8 sts.

Rnd 1: [K1, m1L] around.
Rnd 2: Knit.
Rnd 3: [K2, m1L] around.
Rnds 4–5: Knit.
Rnd 6: [K3, m1L] around.
Rnds 7–9: Knit.
Rnd 10: [K4, m1L] around.
Rnds 11–14: Knit.
Rnd 15: [K5, m1L] around.
Rnds 16–20: Knit.
Rnd 21: [K6, m1L] around.
Rnds 22–27: Knit.
Rnd 28: [K7, m1L] around.

Return to the provisional cast on, draw tail through the cast-on stitches, pull tightly to close, and darn in the end.

SWIRL TOE

To work this toe, the number of stitches for the foot must be divisible by 4.

Using a provisional cast on and leaving a tail of yarn at least 4" long, start with 8 stitches. Join to work in the round.

Rnd 1: [Knit to next marker, m1L] around. 4 sts increased.

Repeat this round until you have approximately S × 0.5 sts on the needles.

Rnd 1: [Knit to next marker, m1L] around. 4 sts increased.
Rnd 2: Knit.

Repeat these 2 rounds until you have S sts on the needles. Return to the provisional cast on, draw tail through the cast-on stitches, pull tightly to close, and darn in the end.

SHORT-ROW TOE

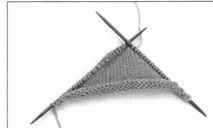

For a narrow toe: Determine S/6 sts. Round up or down until it is a whole number. Let's call this T.

For a medium toe: Determine S/4 sts. Round up or down until it is a whole number. Let's call this T.

For a wide toe: Determine S/3 sts. Round up or down until it is a whole number. Let's call this T.

Using a provisional cast on, start with S × 0.5 stitches. (Ex.: 32 sts) Purl those stitches.

Setup Row 1: Sl1, knit to 1 st from end, m1L. Turn.
Setup Row 2: Sl1, purl to 1 st from end, m1P. Turn.

Row 1: Sl1, knit 1 fewer st than you purled the row before, m1L. Turn.
Row 2: Sl1, purl 1 fewer st than you knit the row before, m1P. Turn.

Repeat until the number of sts you purl is around T.

Turning Row 1: Sl1, knit 1 fewer st than you purled the row before, ssk, k1. Turn.
Turning Row 2: Sl1, purl the same number of sts as you knit the row before, p2tog, p1. Turn.

Row 1: Sl1, knit 1 more st than you purled the row before, ssk, k1. Turn.
Row 2: Sl1, purl 1 more st than you knit the row before, p2tog, p1. Turn.

Repeat until you have worked all of your stitches. You should have the original number of cast-on stitches on the needle. Pm for the beginning of the round. Knit back across the live stitches. Place another marker. Pick up stitches from the original cast on. Join to work in the round.

TRAINING WHEEL TOE

This toe combines elements of the short-row toe and the wedge toe. I wrote it because a few of my friends expressed the desire to work toe-up socks, but found working the first few rounds to be horribly fiddly. You can avoid Judy's Magic Cast On and the first few rounds of a wedge toe by using this method instead.

Tip: I like to have a smaller, sharper needle at hand for working my lifted increases. It greatly reduces the stress on the yarn and my hands.

Each toe begins with a certain number of stitches to be cast on, using a provisional cast on. This needs to be a whole number. If S/2 is odd, it should be odd. If S/2 is even, it should be even.

The following setup is then worked:

Setup Row 1: Purl all sts.

Shorter Row 1: Knit to 1 st from end, m1L. Turn.
Shorter Row 2: Sl1, purl to 1 st from end, m1P. Turn.

Turning Row 1: Sl1, knit 1 fewer st than you purled the row before, ssk, k1, turn.

Turning Row 2: Sl1, purl the same number of sts as you knit the row before, p2tog, p1. Turn.

You should have the original number of cast-on stitches on the needle. Pm for the beginning of the round. Knit back across the live stitches. Place another marker. Pick up and knit stitches from the original cast on. Join to work in the round.

Short Version

Cast on approximately (S × 0.15) + 2 sts.

Ex.: (64 × 0.15) + 2 = 9.6 + 2 = about 12

Work setup section. Continue as for a Short Wedge Toe, starting with "Repeat Round 1 until …"

Medium Version

Cast on approximately (S × 0.1) + 2 sts.

Ex.: (64 × 0.1) + 2 = 6.4 + 2 = about 8

Work setup section. Continue as for a Medium Wedge Toe, starting with "Repeat Round 1 until …"

Long Version

Cast on approximately (S × 0.1) + 2 sts.

Work setup section. Continue as for a Long Wedge Toe, starting with "Repeat Round 1 until …"

Toe-Up Heels

GUSSETS … AND WHY I THINK ABOUT THEM TOO MUCH

In top-down construction, the heel flap is worked as a mostly free-standing piece of knitting, and stitches are picked up from the edges of the flap for the gusset. "Gusset" is really just a fancy term for a triangular bit of knitting that's used to change the size and shape of a piece. It adds circumference to a sock so that it fits around the arch of

TRAINING WEDGE TOES

Training wheel toe, starting.

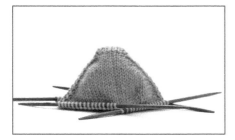

Training wheel toe, complete, as medium wedge toe.

the foot, which is 15–25 percent bigger around than the circumference of the ball of the foot. Top-down socks have gussets that are made using decreases. Toe-up socks have gussets that are made using increases.

Once you think about things this way, the flap-and-gusset heel becomes a lot easier to turn on its head. The heel flap isn't worked on its own, but is made as a series of short rows that are all the same length. What would be picked-up stitches from the edge of the top-down heel flap must instead be live stitches ready to decrease and close the toe-up heel flap to the side of the sock.

By the way, there's also no real reason that gusset stitches are increased or decreased only on the side of the foot. The top, the bottom, or heck, the whole darn foot of the sock could all be used for that just as easily.

FLAP-AND-GUSSET HEELS

No matter the heel turn, after you have finished it, you need to have enough stitches to work the heel flap and stitches for the instep of the sock.

Remember that X, the number of heel flap stitches, is S/2. S is the total number of stitches worked for the foot/ leg of the sock.

To work the heel flap, you need the stitches that actually make the flap (X) and stitches that will be decreased to close the heel flap to the sock.

These are the *Alice through the Looking Glass* versions of stitches that would be picked up from the edge of a heel flap in a top-down sock. It is possible to customize the heel flap length with toe-up socks, just as with top-down socks. But, unless you have a good reason to need more or fewer heel flap rows, you should have as many of these stitches as you have heel-flap stitches (X).

After the heel turn and before the heel flap is worked, we need the heel flap stitches (X), plus the stitches needed to attach the heel flap to the sock (X), and the stitches left for the instep (X). It comes out to 1.5 times the number of stitches on the foot/leg of the sock. This is the total number of stitches needed after the heel turn is worked, but before the heel flap is made. (Toe-up socks without gussets will be a bit more simple to design. Just determine how long the foot should be before the heel is added and skip to step #5 on page 42.)

This all means that when you increase stitches for your gusset, how many stitches you need will depend on what kind of heel turn you are using. You can fudge a little here or there, but each heel turn will have its own number of stitches needed for a gusset—and that number is smaller than you might think.

When to Start Gusset Shaping

Remember the foot measurements chart on page 12? That will help a lot right now. Before you begin knitting your sock, you should already know A. Each heel turn and gusset will

TOE-UP HEEL TYPES AND THEIR FEATURES

	picked-up stitches	gusset	short rows	grafting	patterns in the book that use this heel
Round Heel	yes	yes	yes	no	Strie, Procrastinatrix
Half-Handkerchief Heel	yes	yes	yes	no	Mouchoir
Square Heel	yes	yes	yes	no	Checked and Square
Band Heel	yes	sometimes	yes	no	Dyad
Short-Row Heel	no	no	yes	no	Arithmophobia
Joined Heel Flap	yes	no	no	no	
Shaped Joined Heel Flap	yes	no	no	no	Adjoin

have a unique A3, and instructions for calculating it, in rows, are included with every heel in this book. I like to multiply A by the round gauge of my sock to get the total number of rounds needed for the foot, subtract A3, then divide the result by the round gauge to see when I should start gusset shaping.

You could also just divide A3 by the round gauge and start gusset shaping when your sock is that much shorter than A.

> I don't worry too much about "fitting" a multiple-row pattern evenly into the straight portion of the sock foot with toe-up socks. Why? I don't need to, and neither do you. With top-down socks, the last round worked before heel shaping begins matters a lot, because it determines where the last round of the pattern will fall before the toe is worked. In the toe-up world, that round can fall wherever it likes. If an adjustment is needed to complete the pattern repeat, the leg of the sock can simply be made shorter or longer.

OK, Let's Get on with It, Then

These instructions assume that the beginning of the round is on the side of the foot and that the first half of the round, before you begin gusset shaping, is the top of the foot.

Each of these heels is worked using the same steps.

1. Calculate how many gusset stitches are needed.

2. Determine how long the foot should be before gusset shaping starts.

3. Pm X stitches away from the beginning of the round.

4. Shape the gusset:
   Rnd 1: Work to marker, sm, m1R, work to end of rnd, m1L. 2 sts increased.
   Rnd 2: Work all sts.
   Repeat these 2 rnds until you have added all of your gusset stitches.

5. Work the heel turn.

6. Work setup row(s) for the heel flap.

7. Using short-rows that are all the same length, make the heel flap.

The following instructions make a slipped-stitch heel flap:
(WS): Sl1, p(X − 2), p2tog. Turn.
(RS) if X is even: (Sl1, k1) for (X − 2) sts, sl1, ssk. Turn.
(RS) if X is odd: (Sl1, k1) for (X − 1) sts, ssk. Turn.

To make a stockinette-stitch heel flap:
(WS): Sl1, p(X − 2), p2tog. Turn.
(RS): Sl1, k(X − 2), ssk. Turn.

For both:
Repeat these 2 rows until you are 1 stitch away from having the number of leg stitches you want. Work 1 more WS row. Remove the marker that isn't for the beginning of the rnd and continue onto the leg.

SQUARE HEEL

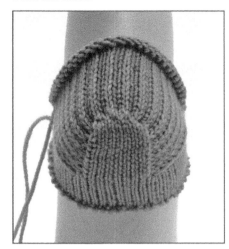

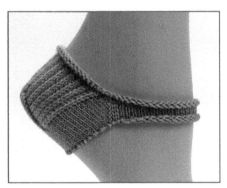

Toe-up square heel with slipped-stitch heel flap. If you are using a set of 5 dpns, 2 more needles could keep you from having to rearrange sts.

Gusset stitches needed: About one-third of the heel flap stitches, but you may need to round by a stitch or two.

If you are using a set of five dpns, two more needles could keep you from having to rearrange stitches.

The heel flap, ultimately, will be divided into thirds. For our example sock of X = 32, that is 11–10–11. Just to keep things from getting super-complicated, let's call the 11 stitches on either side of our (for now) imaginary heel flap the "side strap" and the 10 stitches in the center the heel strap. You need to add as many stitches for the gusset as you will need for the width of the heel strap.

EXAMPLE

The length, in rows, of the gusset and the length of the heel turn, together, will equal the number of stitches needed for the gusset (10) plus the number needed for the heel turn (twice the side-strap stitches, 22).

The gusset and heel turn shaping together are as long in rows as your heel flap is wide in stitches. Begin gusset shaping when the foot of the sock is that amount (32 rounds) shorter than the final desired length.

Work the increases for the gusset.

Heel turn:
Setup Row: Work to the marker, remove it, then work half of your heel flap stitches and all of your heel strap stitches. In other words, work across everything except the last half of your heel flap stitches. (Ex.: 74 – 16 = 58 stitches worked.)

Turn the work. You will continue over just the heel strap stitches. (This is where some spare needles might come in handy.)

(WS): Sl1, purl to end *(ex: p9)*.
(RS): Sl1, knit to end *(ex: k9)*.

Work these 2 rows as many times as you have side-strap stitches *(ex: 22 rows or 11 repeats)*.

Setup Row 1: Pick up all but 1 side-strap stitch from the edge of the piece you just made, pm, pick up that last stitch. Work around the instep, pick up 1 stitch from the other side of your heel strap, pm, then pick up the rest of your side-strap stitches *(ex: 96 sts, total)*.

If your side-strap number is odd:
Setup Row 2: [K1, sl1] to marker (end k1, if you need to), sm, ssk. Turn.

If your side-strap number is even:
Setup Row 2: [Sl1, k1] to marker (end sl1, if you need to), sm, ssk. Turn.

Make the heel flap.

ROUND HEEL

Toe-up round heel with slip-stitch heel flap.

The round heel isn't quite as straight-forward as the square heel, but the very good fit for most people will make it worth the extra effort.

Rows to work the heel turn (let's call this R): R = (X − 4) / 2

I have a formula for how many stitches are needed to work a round-heel gusset. It shouldn't be larger than the number of rows needed to work the heel turn, and it should be at least 10 percent of the original stitches for the foot, but probably not larger than 33 percent. Most of mine are around 28 percent. Is this oddly specific? Yes. But it works. Unlike with a top-down sock, you really need to know how many stitches are needed for the gusset before you begin the gusset increases or, even, the foot, since it determines when you begin gusset shaping.

To see how many gusset stitches you need, take X – R = gusset stitches needed (let's call this G).

- For a 24-stitch heel, you need 14 gusset stitches and 10 rows to work it.
- For a 32-stitch heel, you need 18 gusset stitches and 14 rows to work it.
- For a 36-stitch heel, you need 20 gusset stitches and 16 rows to work it.
- For a 40-stitch heel, you need 22 gusset stitches and 18 rows to work it.

EXAMPLE

The length of the gusset and the length of the heel turn, together, will equal the number of stitches needed for the gusset (18) plus the number needed for the heel turn (14). Also, the number of stitches for the heel flap = number of rounds for gusset shaping + number of rows for heel turn.

Begin gusset shaping when the foot of the sock is that amount (32 rounds) shorter than the final desired length.

Work the increases for the gusset.

Heel turn:
Row 1: Work to marker, remove it, then work across everything except the last half of your heel flap sts. *(Ex.: 82 – 16 = 66 sts worked.)* M1L. Turn.
Row 2: Sl1, pG, m1P. Turn.

Row 3: Sl1, k(G – 1), m1L. Turn.
Row 4: Sl1, p(G – 2), m1P. Turn.

Repeat the last 2 rows, working 1 fewer stitch between increases and turns, until you have worked the number of rows needed for your heel. For the example, this is 14 rows and it ends with:

Row 14: Sl1, p6, m1P. Turn.

Setup Row if X is odd: Sl1, k(G/2), m1L, k(G/2), ssk. Turn.
Setup Row if X is even: Sl1, kG, ssk. Turn.

Make the heel flap.

HALF HANDKERCHIEF HEEL

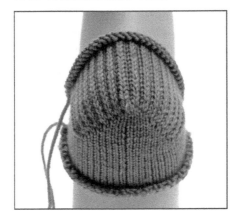

In many ways, the Half Handkerchief Heel is much easier to figure out than a Round Heel, but the instructions are nearly identical.

Gusset stitches needed: X/2 sts.
Rows to work the heel turn: X/2 rows.

The gusset shaping and the heel turn, together, will take as many rows to work as the heel flap is wide, in stitches.

EXAMPLE

Gusset stitches needed: 16 sts.
Rows to work the heel turn: 16 rows.

Begin gusset shaping when the foot of the sock is 32 rounds shorter than the final desired length of the foot.

Shape the gusset.

Heel turn:
Row 1: Work to marker, remove it, then work across everything except the last half of your heel flap sts. *(Ex.: 80 – 16 = 64 sts worked.)* M1L. Turn.
Row 2: Sl1, pG, m1P. Turn.

Row 3: Sl1, k(G – 1), m1L. Turn.
Row 4: Sl1, p(G – 2), m1P. Turn.

Continue in pattern as set, working 1 fewer stitch between increases and turns, until you have worked the number of rows needed for your heel. For the example, this is 16 rows and it ends with:

Row 16: Sl1, p2, m1P. Turn.
Setup Row: Sl1, kG, ssk. Turn.
Make the heel flap.

BAND HEEL WITH GUSSET

This begins in a way that is very similar to the Square Heel, with a very small heel strap.

Gusset stitches needed: X/4 sts. (For a 64-stitch sock, increase to 72 stitches before working the heel.)

Rows to work the heel turn: 3X/4 rows.

The heel and gusset shaping, overall, takes a total of X rows/rounds to work. So, begin gusset shaping when your sock foot is X rows/rounds shorter than desired.

Shape the gusset.

PICKING UP STITCHES FOR BAND HEEL WITH GUSSET

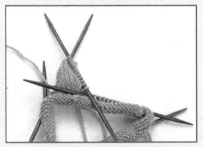

Heel turn:
Setup Row: Work all of the stitches in the round except for half of the heel stitches. *(Ex.: 72 – 16 = 56)* Turn. The strap is X/4 sts wide. *(Ex.: 8 sts)*

Row 1 (WS): Sl1, purl to end of strap. (Ex.: p7) Turn.
Row 2 (RS): Sl1, knit to end of strap. (Ex.: k7) Turn.

Repeat these 2 rows a total of X/4 times. Break yarn. Reattach at the right side of the base of the strap and pick up and knit one stitch for every 2 rows you worked for the strap, kfb, k(strap sts – 2), kfb, pick up and knit 1 stitch for every 2 rows you worked for the strap. *(Ex.: 8 sts, kfb, k6, kfb, pick up and knit 8 sts.)* Slip 1 st back onto the left-hand needle and ssk it to the st next to it. Turn.

Setup Row (WS): Sl1, pm, purl the picked up sts plus 1 more, pm, purl across strap sts, pm, purl the picked up sts (minus 1), pm, p2tog. Turn.

In these last X/2 rows, you have added X/2 sts to your stitch count.

Row 1 (RS): Sl1, sm, knit to marker, m1L, sm, knit to marker, sm, m1R, knit to marker, ssk. Turn.
Row 2 (WS): Sl1, purl to 4th marker, p2tog. Turn.

Repeat these 2 rows until you have (X – 2) sts between the 1st and 4th markers. This is another X/4 sts added and it takes X/4 rows to work. Remove all markers.

Setup Row: Sl1, k(X – 2) sts, ssk. Turn. Make the heel flap.

BAND HEEL WITHOUT GUSSET

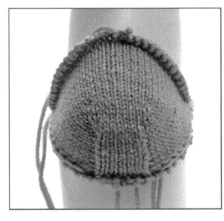

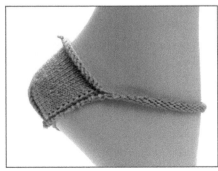

See the information on the Band Heel on page 27.

The heel only takes 3X/4 rows to work, so begin shaping it when your sock is that many rows shorter than desired.

(In the example, this is 24 rows, or just a tiny bit over 2".) This whole process is easiest when X/4 is a whole number.

This heel is worked in three parts:

Part 1
Take (X/4) and mark those off as your center strap stitches at the bottom of the heel. This needs to be a whole number. If X is odd, X/4 is odd. If X is even, X/4 is even. If the beginning of your round is at the side of the toe:

Setup Row (RS): Work (X/2 + X/8) sts. Turn.

Row 1 (WS): Sl1, p[(X/4) – 1]. Turn.
Row 2 (RS): Sl1, k[(X/4) – 1]. Turn.

Example Setup Row (RS): K20. Turn.
Example Row 1 (WS): Sl1, p7. Turn.
Example Row 2 (RS): Sl1, k7. Turn.

Repeat these 2 rows X/4 times, rounding X/4 up to an even number. Break yarn.

Part 2
Reattach at the right side of the base of the strap and pick up and knit 1 stitch for every 2 rows you worked for the strap, kfb, k(strap sts – 2), kfb, pick up and knit 1 stitch for every two rows you worked for the strap. *(Ex.: 8 sts, kfb, k6, kfb, pick up and knit 8 sts.)* Slip 1 st back onto the left-hand needle and ssk it to the stitch next to it. Turn.

Setup Row (WS): Sl1, pm, purl the picked up sts plus 1 more, pm, purl across strap sts, pm, purl the picked up sts (minus 1), pm, p2tog. Turn.

In these last X/2 rows, you have added X/2 sts to your stitch count.

Row 1 (RS): Sl1, sm, knit to marker, m1L, sm, knit to marker, sm, m1R, knit to marker, ssk. Turn.
Row 2 (WS): Sl1, purl to 4th marker, p2tog. Turn.

Repeat these 2 rows until you have (X – 2) sts between the 1st and 4th markers. This is another X/4 sts increased and it takes X/4 rows to work. Remove all markers.

Part 3
Row 1: (RS): Sl1, k(X – 2) sts, ssk.
Turn.
Row 2: (WS): Sl1, p(X – 2) sts, p2tog.
Turn.

Repeat these 2 rows until you have the total number of sts you want for the leg. Continue onto the leg.

Afterthought Heels with Gussets

Please see the afterthought heel section from Chapter 3 (page 29).

This method allows you to work a toe-up sock and decide if you want the heel to be from the top down or the toe up later.

You will need to know how many rows you will need to work the gusset shaping the heel turn for each particular heel before you begin gusset shaping.

Short-Row Heels

Please see the short-row heel section from Chapter 3 (page 33). The instructions are identical whether you are working this heel from the top down or toe up.

Joined Heel Flap

This heel shaping takes S/2 rows to work, so the sock's foot is worked straight until it is as long as it should be, less those S/2 rows. When ready to work the heel, half of the foot stitches are put on hold for the instep. The heel stitches are then worked, alone.

Row 1 (RS): Sl1, knit to end.
Row 2 (WS): Sl1, purl to end.

Work these 2 rows S/2 times. In our example sock, this will be worked over 32 stitches 16 times. The heel stitches are then worked halfway across, the flap is folded in half and the edges are bound off together, grafted or cast off and seamed.

When you are finished, break the yarn, leaving a 6" tail. Starting from the point where you first left off your instep stitches, pick up and knit 1 stitch for every slipped-edge stitch along the top of the heel. You should now be ready to work a new round, if the beginning of your round is at the side of the sock. I like to leave that tail sticking out. It's useful for tidying up the join at the top of the heel bind off, which can sometimes be a bit sloppy.

ZIGZAG BIND OFF

In *Ethnic Socks & Stockings*, Priscilla Gibson-Roberts describes a form of three-needle bind off that she calls the Zigzag bind off, which might be interesting even to knitters who don't want to try this particular heel, because it forms a flat and pretty join.

Designate one side of the heel stitches as side 1 and the other as side 2.

With a spare needle, k1 from side 1, p1 from side 2. Pass the first stitch over the second stitch on your spare needle.

Then, repeat as follows until all stitches are bound off:
Row 1: K1 from side 1, pass the 1st stitch over the 2nd stitch on your spare needle.
Row 2: P1 from side 2, pass the 1st stitch over the 2nd stitch on your spare needle.

Shaped Joined Heel Flap

While the Zigzag bind off is an interesting technique, I do prefer a heel that fits a little more closely to the foot.

Work as for Joined Heel Flap for approximately X × 0.75 rows. *(Ex.: 32 × 0.75 = 24)*

Finish that last 25 percent of rows with shaping.

If X is an even number:
Pm at X/2 heel stitches.

(RS): Sl1, knit to 2 sts before marker, k2tog, ssk, knit to end.
(WS): Sl1, purl to end.

If X is an odd number:
Pm at X/2 heel stitches, rounding X/2 down to a whole number.

(RS): Sl1, knit to 2 sts before marker, k2tog, k1, ssk, knit to end.
(WS): Sl1, purl to end.

Repeat these 2 rows until you have increased that last 25 percent to the length of the heel flap. (Round down if you need to. For our example, this would be 8 rows.) On the last WS row, only work up to the marker. Fold the work with the wrong sides together and use a Zigzag bind off to close. (If X is odd, use sl1, purl to 2 sts before the marker, p2tog as your last WS row.)

When you are finished, break the yarn, leaving a 6" tail. Starting from the point where you first left off your instep stitches, pick up and knit 1 stitch for every slipped-edge stitch along the top of the heel. You should now be ready to work a new round. I like to leave that tail sticking out. It's useful for tidying up the join at the top of the heel bind-off, which can sometimes be a bit sloppy.

When X is odd, you may end up with a slightly different number of stitches after the heel shaping than you had before the shaping. If so, aim to make the number a little higher rather than a little lower and decrease away your extra stitches in the first few rounds of the leg, in whatever location you think will look the best.

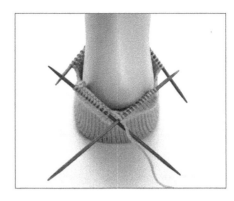

Shaped joined heel flap on my Adjoined Socks, ready to join.

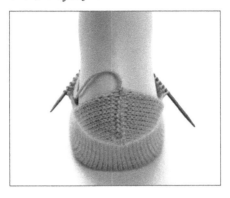

Shaped joined heel flap, closed with Zigzag bind off.

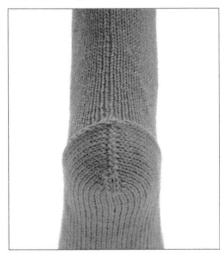

Back of final sock.

The Leg and a Good Bind Off

Unless I have a stylistic reason not to, I like to work my sock legs in all ribbing. This makes them more stretchy, less likely to fall down—and more comfortable, in my opinion. (See Part I, page 18, for more information about sizing your leg to fit properly.)

Once you have finished knitting the leg, I like Jeny's Surprisingly Stretchy Bind Off <knitty.com/ISSUEfall09/FEATjssbo.php>, but any bind off that is stretchy enough for the sock to get over the foot will work. Techknitter wrote a wonderful series of blog posts in 2011 about bind offs <techknitting.blogspot.com/2011/11/stretchiest-and-easiest-cast-on-and.html>. I used her "stretchiest" bind off in my Tootsie Socks <knitty.com/ISSUEss12/PATTtootsie.php>.

OTHER CONSTRUCTIONS, AVENUES AND DIVERSIONS

Cookie A

Cookie A might be the most well-known sock designer. Her designs are complex and interesting to knit, but fit can sometimes be an issue, as her design elements and stitch patterns can limit customization.

Cat Bordhi

Cat Bordhi has continued Elizabeth Zimmermann's proud tradition of thinking way outside of the box, especially in socks. Her Sweet Tomato Heel is a complete re-imagining of short-row shaping.

Lisa Grossman, or the Tsarina of Tsocks

Lisa Grossman takes socks in interesting, new directions. Her "Frankenshteek" socks are especially fun and give the intrepid knitter a fear to face—and conquer.

Hunter Hammersen

The awesome creative force behind Panstville Press <pantsvillepress.com>, Hunter Hammersen's sock designs are works of art that stretch the limits of fit and aesthetics.

Katherine Misegades

A former instructor of nurses, Katherine uses her knowledge of anatomy to create unusual, very fun-to-knit socks. Her instructions are invariably clear and straightforward, too. Check out her Sock Workshop <katherinemisegades.wordpress.com/sock-workshop> and find her on Ravelry.

Susan Glinert Stevens

Mostly known by her online moniker "Fleegle," her Fleegle heel is a revolutionary look at toe-up sock heels. It is well worth mastering. You can find her on her blog <fleeglesblog.blogspot.com/> or on Ravelry.

Elizabeth Zimmermann

I think of Elizabeth Zimmermann as the Architect of Knitting. As such, many of her sock constructions are unique, fun to knit, and go way beyond anything I've discussed so far. In particular, her Sideways Socks, Moccasin Socks, Wearable Art Stockings and Stockings with Form-Fitted Arch are all very much worth hunting down and knitting.

Patterns
Patterns
Patterns
Patterns
Patterns
Patterns

Some General Notes about the Patterns

DPNs, Magic Loop, and Markers

I'm a big fan of needle-neutral patterns. All of my patterns are written so that they can be worked with any kind of needle configuration—magic loop, two circulars, short circulars or (my favorite) double-pointed needles (DPNs).

I use stitch markers to keep track of where I am on a sock. This can sometimes be awkward when using DPNs and even the magic loop method. So, I cheat a little bit and use the break between needles as a marker. For example, when the pattern reads "place a marker for the beginning of the round," I might actually arrange or rearrange stitches so that the last stitch in the round is on one needle and the first stitch in the round is on the next needle.

Custom Fitting and "Adjustable Sizes"

Finished leg length and finished foot length are marked as "adjustable to fit" in these patterns. Shoe sizes can be a good place to start, but there is no substitute for careful measuring.

Measure the recipient's foot when she or he is standing, preferably with the back of the heel touching a wall, so you can measure from the wall to the tip of the longest toe. If you are working alone, this will remind you of yoga class, so it really is easier if you have help.

Take this measurement and multiply it by 0.9 to see how long the sock's foot should be.

Leg length is more a matter of preference than anything, but most socks work well if the leg is at least as long as the foot. If your sock's leg is much longer than 8"/20cm or so, you may want to check and make sure the top of the sock won't be too tight around the calf.

Most of the patterns in this book can be worked with the stitch counts I have given, but also using your own gauge and measurements.

Work a gauge swatch in the round with the yarn, needles, and stitch pattern you plan on using for the sock. Measure your gauge over 4"/10cm, if possible.

Measure the intended recipient's foot in two ways:

- Circumference at the ball of the foot or the largest part of the foot near the ball of the foot.

- Length of foot from back of heel to tip of longest toe.

Take each of these numbers and multiply them by 0.9. These will be the key measurements for your sock.

Now convert circumference to stitches:

- Circumference of sock, in inches or cm.

- Circumference of sock, in stitches (the above number, times your gauge).

Take a look at your "circumference, in stitches" number. This number is S, but you may need to round up or down. Each pattern will say if S has to be divisible by a certain number for the pattern to work. If you end up rounding by more than ¼"/0.65 cm to get the math to work, proceed with caution. If possible, make an in-the-round gauge

swatch over S stitches that is at least 2"/5 cm long and have the recipient try it on.

X is S / 2.

Length of sock, in inches or cm = L

When you see "U" in the instructions, it means that you should determine that number/measurement.

Yarn Amounts

But, how much yarn will you need? I think this question is what kept me from designing my own knits for so many years. Hopefully, your custom size will fall between the written sizes for this book. Check the yarn amounts needed for the size nearest to yours, but always overestimate. Leftovers are better than incomplete socks!

Adjusting for Your Round Gauge

In all of the patterns in this book, I assume that you are working at 11 rounds per inch, but I also give you the length measurement needed, in rounds or rows. If you are not getting 11 rounds per inch, you will have to work a small conversion at those moments.

Carefully count 4 inches worth of rows. Divide this number by 4 to find your row gauge.

For example, the heel shaping on my Adjoin socks takes 28 (30, 32, 34, 38, X) rows to work. Take the number of rows for your size and divide it by your row gauge. When your sock is that much shorter than you want it to be, begin working the heel shaping.

Strie, Top Down

SIZES

Women's XS (Women's S, Women's M/ Men's S, Women's L/Men's M, Men's L, Adjustable Size)

FINISHED MEASUREMENTS

Foot circumference: 7 (7½, 8, 8½, 9½, U)"/18 (19, 20.5, 21.5, 24, U) cm

Finished leg length: adjustable to fit
Finished foot length: adjustable to fit

MATERIALS

Simply Socks Yarn Company Simply Sock Yarn (80% superwash wool, 20% nylon; 175yd/160m per 50g skein); color: #620 Cerulean (Women's M) and #260 Adobe (Child's size 7); 2 (2, 2, 2, 3, U) skeins

US#1 (2.25 mm) needles or size needed to achieve gauge

3 stitch markers
Yarn needle

GAUGE

32 sts and 44 rnds = 4"/10 cm in both stockinette stitch and Single Garter Rib stitch

SPECIAL STITCHES

Single Garter Rib

(Worked over 2 sts in the round)
Rnd 1: [K1, p1] around.
Rnd 2: Knit.

PATTERN

To work out your own custom sizing to use in the instructions that follow, see page 52.

Cast On and Leg

CO 56 (60, 64, 68, 76, S) sts. Distribute sts among needles as you prefer, and join without twisting to work in the round.

Work [k1, p1] ribbing for 2"/5 cm.

*S*TRIE MEANS "STRIPE," "GROOVE," OR "GORE" in French, so it seems like the perfect name for these very simple, garter-stitch-ribbed socks with French heels and wedge toes. This version is worked from the top down.

Work Single Garter Rib until the leg measures 2½ (2¾, 3, 3, 3½, [X/11])"/6.5 (7, 7.5, 8, 8.5, [X/4.4]) cm is approx. 2"/5 cm shorter than your desired length to bottom of heel, ending with a Rnd 1.

Heel Flap

For the heel flap, you will work back and forth over only the first half of your stitches: 28 (30, 32, 34, 38, X) sts. Leave the others on hold.

Row 1 (RS): [Sl1, k1] 14 (15, 16, 17, 19, X/2) times.
Row 2 (WS): Sl1, purl to end.

Rep these 2 rows 13 (14, 15, 16, 18, A) more times.

Heel Turn

Row 1 (RS): Sl1, k14 (15, 16, 17, 19, X/2), ssk, k1. Turn.
Row 2 (WS): Sl1, p5, p2tog, p1. Turn.
Row 3: Sl1, k6, ssk, k1. Turn.
Row 4: Sl1, p7, p2tog, p1. Turn.

Continue in patt as set, working one more stitch before the decrease in each row, until you have worked all of the heel stitches, then work one final WS row as follows: Sl1, purl to last 3 sts, p2tog, p1. 16 (18, 18, 20, 22, G) sts on the needles. K8 (9, 9, 10, 11, G/2) and pm for start of rnd.

Gusset

Knit across the remaining half of the heel sts, pick up sts for the right side of the gusset by picking up and knitting one stitch through each slipped-stitch

chain on the edge of the heel flap for 14 (15, 16, 17, 19, X/2) sts, pm for the start of the instep.

Work across instep in Single Garter Ridge as established, pm, pick up 14 (15, 16, 17, 19, X/2) sts for the left side of the gusset in the same way as you did for the right, knit to end of rnd. 72 (78, 82, 88, 98, B) sts.

Rnd 1: Knit to 2 sts before the instep marker, k2tog, work Single Garter Ridge to marker, ssk, knit to end of rnd. 2 sts decreased.
Rnd 2: Knit to instep marker, work Single Garter Ridge to marker, knit to end of rnd.

Rep these 2 rnds until the sock has the same number of sts as it had on the leg, 56 (60, 64, 68, 76, S) sts.

The Rest of the Foot

Once the gusset decreases are finished, leave the stitch markers in place, and continue to work only Rnd 2 until the foot of the sock is as long as you want, less the length needed for the toe, as follows:

If you are working the Short Wedge Toe, start toe shaping when your sock is 1½ (1½, 1¾, 1¾, 2, U)"/3.5 (4, 4, 4.5, 5, U) cm or 16 (17, 18, 19, 22, 0.275 × S) rnds shorter than the desired length of the sock.

If you are working the Medium Wedge Toe, start toe shaping when your sock is 1¾ (1¾, 2, 2, 2¼, U)"/4 (4.5, 5, 5, 5.5, U) cm or 18 (19, 21, 22, 24, 0.325 × S) rnds shorter than the desired length of the sock.

If you are working the Long Wedge Toe, start toe shaping when your sock is 2¼ (2¼, 2¾, 2¾, 3, U)"/5.5 (6, 6.5, 7, 7.5, U) cm or 25 (26, 29, 30, 33, 0.45 × S) rnds shorter than the desired length of the sock.

Toe

The pattern stitch ends here. The toe is worked in stockinette stitch.

SHORT WEDGE TOE

Rnd 1: [Knit to 2 sts before marker, k2tog, sm, ssk] twice, knit to end of rnd.
Rnd 2: Knit.

Rep Rnds 1 and 2 until you have 32 (36, 36, 40, 44, I) sts on the needles. Then, rep only Rnd 1 until you have 16 (16, 20, 20, 20, K) sts on the needles. Knit to marker, graft rem sts closed.

MEDIUM WEDGE TOE

Rnd 1: [Knit to 2 sts before marker, k2tog, sm, ssk] twice, knit to end of rnd.
Rnd 2: Knit.

Rep Rnds 1 and 2 until you have 28 (32, 32, 36, 40, ~X) sts on the needles. Then, rep only Rnd 1 until you have 12 (12, 12, 12, 16, J) sts on the needles. Knit to marker, graft rem sts closed.

LONG WEDGE TOE

Rnd 1: [Knit to 3 sts before marker, k2tog, k1, sm, k1, ssk] twice, knit to end of rnd.
Rnds 2 and 3: Knit.

Rep Rnds 1–3 until you have 28 (32, 32, 36, 40, ~X) sts on the needles. Then, rep only Rnd 1 until you have 12 (12, 12, 12, 16, J) sts on the needles. Knit to marker, graft rem sts closed.

Finishing

Weave in all ends and block gently.

WORKING OUT CUSTOM SIZING FOR STRIE, TOP DOWN

See page 49 for help with using this table. S must be divisible by 4.

Variable	How to calculate that variable	Write your result below
A	(X / 2) − 1	
R	(X − 4) / 2 Round down, if needed, so that R is an even number.	
G	X − R	
B	S + G	
I	S × 0.6 Round to nearest multiple of 4.	
J	S × 0.2 Round to nearest multiple of 4.	
K	S × 0.3 Round to nearest multiple of 4.	
U	Use U to figure out the length of your toe shaping For Short Toe: U = (0.275 × S) / your round gauge For Medium Toe: U = (0.325 × S) / your round gauge For Long Toe: U = (0.45 × S) / your round gauge	

Women's Medium, in Cerulean.

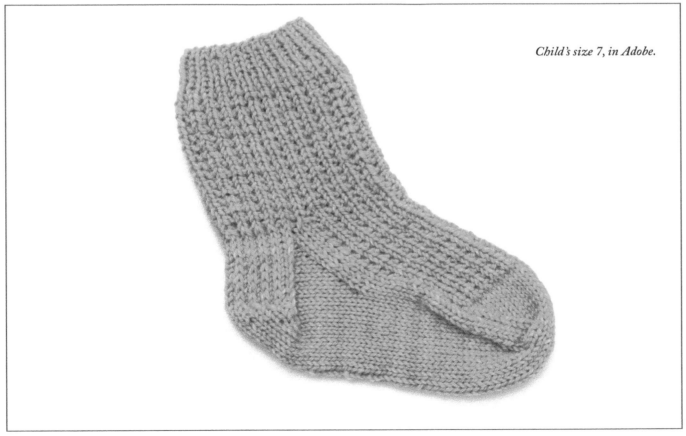

Child's size 7, in Adobe.

Strie, Toe Up

SIZES

Women's XS (Women's S, Women's M/Men's S, Women's L/Men's M, Men's L, Adjustable Size); shown in size Women's M

FINISHED MEASUREMENTS

Foot circumference: 7 (7½, 8, 8½, 9½, U)"/18 (19, 20.5, 21.5, 24, U) cm

Finished leg length: adjustable to fit
Finished foot length: adjustable to fit

MATERIALS

Simply Socks Yarn Company Simply Sock Yarn (80% superwash wool, 20% nylon; 175 yds/160m per 50g skein); color: #410 Golden or #350 Bittersweet; 2 (2, 2, 2, 3, U) skeins

US#1 (2.25 mm) needles or size needed to achieve gauge

3 stitch markers
Yarn needle

I like to have a smaller, sharper needle at hand for working my lifted increases. It greatly reduces the stress on the yarn and my hands.

GAUGE

32 sts and 44 rnds = 4"/10 cm in stockinette stitch

PATTERN

To work out your own custom sizing to use in the instructions that follow, see page 56.

Cast On and Toe

Choose the shape of toe you want to use. If you don't have a favorite, see page 13 for tips.

Women's Medium in Bittersweet.

SHORT WEDGE TOE

CO 16 (20, 20, 20, 20, K) sts, using Judy's Magic Cast On. Knit 1 rnd, placing a marker for beginning of rnd and another one halfway around your toe.

Rnd 1: K1, m1L, knit to 1 st before marker, m1R, k1, sm, k1, m1L, knit to 1 st before end of rnd, m1R, k1. 4 sts increased.
Rep this rnd until you have 32 (36, 36, 40, 44, I) sts on the needles.

Rnd 1: K1, m1L, knit to 1 st before marker, m1R, k1, sm, k1, m1L, knit to 1 st before end of rnd, m1R, k1. 4 sts increased.
Rnd 2: Knit.

Rep these 2 rnds until you have 56 (60, 64, 68, 76, S) sts on the needles.

MEDIUM WEDGE TOE

CO 12 (12, 12, 16, 16, J) sts, using Judy's Magic Cast On. Pm for beginning of rnd and another one halfway around your toe.

Rnd 1: K1, m1L, knit to 1 st before the marker, m1R, k1, sm, k1, m1L, knit to 1 st before the end of the rnd, m1R, k1. 4 sts increased.
Rep this rnd until you have 28 (32, 32, 36, 40, ~X) sts on the needles.

Rnd 1: K1, m1L, knit to 1 st before marker, m1R, k1, sm, k1, m1L, knit to 1 st before end of rnd, m1R, k1. 4 sts increased.
Rnd 2: Knit.

Rep these 2 rnds until you have 56 (60, 64, 68, 76, S) sts on the needles.

LONG WEDGE TOE

CO 12 (12, 12, 16, 16, J) sts, using Judy's Magic Cast On. Pm for beginning of rnd and another one halfway around your toe.

Rnd 1: K1, m1L, knit to 1 st before marker, m1R, k1, sm, k1, m1L, knit to 1 st before end of rnd, m1R, k1. 4 sts increased.
Rep this rnd until you have 28 (32, 32, 36, 40, ~X) sts on the needles.

Rnd 1: K1, m1L, knit to 1 st before marker, m1R, k1, sm, k1, m1L, knit to 1 st before end of rnd, m1R, k1. 4 sts increased.
Rnds 2–3: Knit.

Rep Rnds 1–3 until you have 56 (60, 64, 68, 76, S) sts on the needles.

The Rest of the Foot

You now have 28 (30, 32, 34, 38, X) sts each on instep and sole. Leave stitch markers in place, and continue:

Rnd 1: Work [k1, p1] to end-of-instep marker, knit to end of rnd.
Rnd 2: Knit.

Rep these 2 rnds until foot of sock is as long as you want, less the length needed for the gusset and heel shaping: 2½ (2¾, 3, 3, 3½, X/11)"/6.5 (7, 7.5, 8, 8.5, X/4.4) cm or 28 (30, 32, 34, 38, X) rows long. Stop after working a Rnd 2.

Gusset

Rnd 1: Work patt as set to the marker, m1L, knit to end of rnd, m1R. 2 sts increased.
Rnd 2: Knit.

Rep the last 2 rnds until you have added 16 (18, 18, 20, 22, G) sts; 72 (78, 82, 88, 98, B) sts total.

Heel Turn

Set-up Row (RS): Work in patt as set to marker, remove marker, k30 (33, 34, 37, 41, C) sts, m1L. Turn.

Row 2 (WS): Sl1, p16 (18, 18, 20, 22, G) sts, m1pR. Turn.
Row 3: Sl1, k15 (17, 17, 19, 21, G – 1) sts, m1L. Turn.
Row 4: Sl1, p14 (16, 16, 18, 20, G – 2) sts, m1P. Turn.

Continue in patt as set, working 1 less stitch between increases and turns, until you have worked 12 (12, 14, 14, 16, R) rows. 84 (90, 96, 102, 114, B + R) sts on the needles.

Heel Flap

Set-up Row 1 (RS): Sl1, k16 (18, 18, 20, 22, G) sts, ssk. Turn.
Set-up Row 2 (WS): Sl1, p26 (28, 30, 32, 36, X – 2) sts, p2tog. Turn.

Row 1 (RS): [Sl1, k1] 12 (13, 14, 15, 17, A) times, sl1, ssk. Turn.
Row 2 (WS): Sl1, p26 (28, 30, 32, 36, X – 2) sts, p2tog. Turn.

Rep these 2 rows 12 (13, 14, 15, 17, A) times more. 56 (60, 64, 68, 76, S) sts on the needles.

Remove the marker that isn't for the beginning of the round and continue with the leg.

Leg and Bind Off

Rnd 1: Knit.
Rnd 2: [K1, p1] around.

Rep these 2 rnds until leg is as long as you like, less 2"/5 cm.

Work [k1, p1] ribbing for 2"/5 cm.

BO. I like Jeny's Surprisingly Stretchy Bind Off, but any bind off that is stretchy enough for the sock to get over the foot will work. Please see page 47 for more information about bind offs for toe-up socks.

Finishing

Weave in all ends and block gently.

WORKING OUT CUSTOM SIZING FOR STRIE, TOE UP

See page 49 for help with using this table. S must be divisible by 4.

Variable	How to calculate that variable	Write your result below
A	(X / 2) – 2	
R	(X – 4) / 2 Round down, if needed, so that R is an even number.	
G	X – R	
B	S + G	
I	S × 0.6 Round to nearest multiple of 4.	
J	S × 0.2 Round to nearest multiple of 4.	
K	S × 0.3 Round to nearest multiple of 4.	
C	(X / 2) + G	

Women's Medium
in Golden.

Mouchoir, Top Down

SIZES

Women's XS (Women's M/Men's S, Men's M/L, Adjustable Size); shown in size Women's M

FINISHED MEASUREMENTS

Foot circumference: 7 (8, 9, U)"/18 (20.5, 23, U) cm

Finished leg length: adjustable to fit
Finished foot length: adjustable to fit

MATERIALS

Simply Socks Yarn Company Simply Sock Yarn (80% superwash wool, 20% nylon; 175 yds/160m per 50g skein); color: #735 Lavender; 2 (2, 3, U) skeins

US#1 (2.25 mm) needles or size needed to achieve gauge

2 stitch markers
Yarn needle

GAUGE

32 sts and 44 rnds = 4"/10 cm in both stockinette stitch and Mouchoir stitch (gently blocked)

SPECIAL STITCHES

Mouchoir Stitch

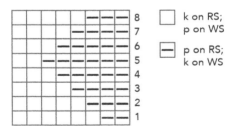

☐	k on RS; p on WS
▬	p on RS; k on WS

(Worked over 8 sts in the round.)
Rnd 1: P2, k6.
Rnd 2: P3, k5.
Rnd 3: P4, k4.
Rnd 4: P5, k3.
Rnd 5: P6, k2.
Rnd 6: P5, k3.
Rnd 7: P4, k4.
Rnd 8: P3, k5.
Rep Rnds 1-8 for patt.

*M*OUCHOIR MEANS "HANDKERCHIEF" in French. This sock has a half-handkerchief heel and a simple stitch pattern to match. This version is knit from the top down and has a round toe, which requires no grafting.

I love this simple stitch pattern, but it does limit sizing options a bit. I hope you can forgive me.

PATTERN

Cast On and Leg

CO 56 (64, 72, S) sts. Distribute sts among your needles as you prefer, and join without twisting to work in the round.

Work in [k1, p1] ribbing for 2"/5 cm.

Next rnd: Work Mouchoir Stitch 7 (8, 9, F) times around.

Continue in patt as set until leg is 2½ (3, 3¼, X/11)"/6.5 (7.5, 8, X/4.4) cm less than your desired final sock. Write down the number of the last patt round worked when you stop.

Heel Flap

For sizes Women's XS, Men's M/L and when F is an odd number: Remove marker for start of rnd, k2, replace marker. This is the new start of the rnd.

All sizes:
For the heel flap, you will work back and forth over only the first half of your sts: 28 (32, 36, X) sts. Leave the others on hold.

Eye of Partridge stitch:
Row 1 (RS): [Sl1, k1] 14 (16, 18, X/2) times.
Row 2 (WS): Sl1, p27 (31, 35, X–1).
Row 3: Sl1, k2, sl1, [k1, sl1] 11 (13, 15, A) times, k2.
Row 4: Sl1, p27 (31, 35, X–1).

WORKING OUT CUSTOM SIZING FOR MOUCHOIR, TOP DOWN

See page 49 for help with using this table. S must be divisible by 8.

Variable	How to calculate that variable	Write your result below
X	S/2	
A	(X / 2) – 3	
B	(X / 4) – 1	
C	(X / 2) – 1	
D	S + (X / 2)	
E	X – 4	
F	S / 8	

Rep these 4 rows 6 (7, 8, B) times more.

Half-Handkerchief Heel Turn

Row 1 (RS): Sl1, k13 (15, 17, C) sts, ssk, k1. Turn.
Row 2 (WS): Sl1, p1, p2tog, p1. Turn.
Row 3: Sl1, k2, ssk, k1. Turn.
Row 4: Sl1, p3, p2tog, p1. Turn.

Continue in patt as set, working 1 more stitch before the decrease in each row, until you have worked all of the heel sts. Note: In the final 2 rows you will turn after the decrease, as there are no more stitches to work. 14 (16, 18, X/2) sts rem on the heel.

K7 (8, 9, F) and pm for start of rnd.

Gusset

With RS facing, knit across rem half of the heel sts, pick up sts for the right side of the gusset by picking up and knitting 1 stitch through each slipped-stitch chain on the edge of the heel flap for 14 (16, 18, X/2) sts, pm for start of instep.

For sizes Women's XS, Men's M/L and when S/8 is an odd number:
K2, work next rnd of Mouchoir Stitch (check your notes to see where you left off), beginning at the 3rd stitch of the patt then repeating across for 24 (–, 32, E) sts, p2, pm for end of instep, pick up 14 (–, 18, X/2) sts for the left side of the gusset in the same way as you did for the right, knit to end of rnd. 70 (–, 90, D) sts.

Rnd 1: Knit to 2 sts before marker, k2tog, k2, work Mouchoir Stitch as established to 2 sts from marker, p2, ssk, knit to end of rnd. 2 sts decreased.
Rnd 2: Knit to marker, k2, work Mouchoir Stitch to 2 sts from marker, p2, knit to end of rnd.

All other sizes:
Work next rnd of Mouchoir Stitch (check your notes to see where you left off) across instep, pm, pick up – (16, –,

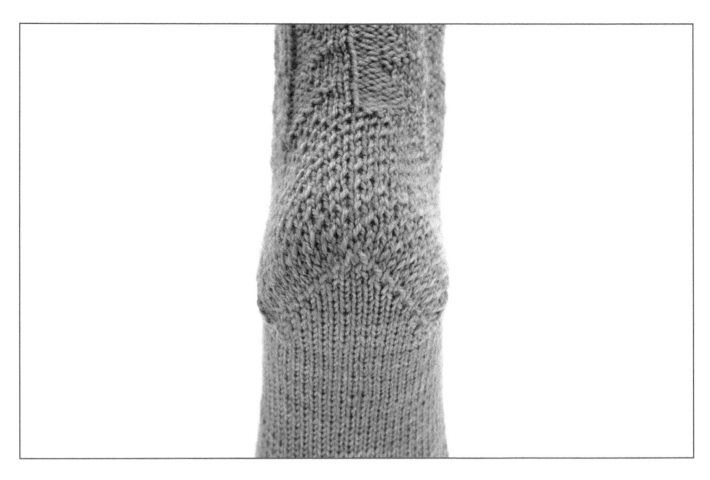

X/2) sts for left side of the gusset in the same way as you did for the right, knit to end of rnd. – (80, –, D) sts.

Rnd 1: Knit to 2 sts before marker, k2tog, work Mouchoir Stitch to marker, ssk, knit to end of rnd. 2 sts decreased.
Rnd 2: Knit to marker, work Mouchoir Stitch to marker, knit to end of rnd.

All sizes:
Rep these 2 rnds until sock has the same number of sts as it had on the leg, 56 (64, 72, S) sts.

The Rest of the Foot

Once gusset decreases are finished, leave stitch markers in place, and rep only Rnd 2 as above until the foot of the sock is as long as you want, less the length needed for the toe.

Start toe shaping when your sock is 2½"/6.5 cm or 28 rnds shorter than the desired length of the sock. Mouchoir Stitch is 8 rnds long, which is almost

¾"/2 cm. If you finish a stitch patt repeat and don't have 8 more rnds to go before you want to begin toe shaping, simply rep only Rnd 1 of the patt stitch until you are finished. The purl sts can be little sticks to wave your hankies on.

Round Toe

The pattern stitch ends here. The toe is worked in stockinette stitch.

Rnd 1: [K6, k2tog] around. 49 (56, 63, F×7) sts.
Rnds 2–7: Knit.

Rnd 8: [K5, k2tog] around. 42 (48, 54, F×6) sts.
Rnds 9–13: Knit.

Rnd 14: [K4, k2tog] around. 35 (40, 45, F×5) sts.
Rnds 15–18: Knit.

Rnd 19: [K3, k2tog] around. 28 (32, 36, F×4) sts.
Rnds 20–22: Knit.

Rnd 23: [K2, k2tog] around. 21 (24, 27, F×3) sts.
Rnds 24–25: Knit.

Rnd 26: [K1, k2tog] around. 14 (16, 18, F×2) sts.
Rnd 27: Knit.

Rnd 28: K2tog around. 7 (8, 9, F) sts.

Finishing

Break yarn, leaving a 6"/15cm tail. With a darning needle, thread yarn through rem sts. Go through twice, if you want the extra security. Pull the stitches tight, bring the yarn to the inside of the sock and weave the tail in.

Weave in all ends and block gently.

Mouchoir, Toe Up

SIZES

Women's XS (Women's M/Men's S, Men's M/L, Adjustable Size); shown in size Women's M

FINISHED MEASUREMENTS

Foot circumference: 7 (8, 9, U)"/18 (20.5, 23,U) cm

Finished leg length: adjustable to fit
Finished foot length: adjustable to fit

MATERIALS

Simply Socks Yarn Company Simply Sock Yarn (80% superwash wool, 20% nylon; 175 yds/160m per 50g skein); color: #735 Lavender; 2 (2, 3, U) skeins

US#1 (2.25 mm) needles or size needed to achieve gauge

3 stitch markers
Yarn needle

I like to have a smaller, sharper needle at hand for working my lifted increases. It greatly reduces the stress on the yarn and my hands.

GAUGE

32 sts and 44 rnds = 4"/10 cm in stockinette or Mouchoir stitch (gently blocked)

SPECIAL STITCHES

Mouchoir Stitch

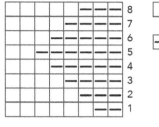

k on RS; p on WS

p on RS; k on WS

(Worked over 8 sts in the round)
Rnd 1: P2, k6.
Rnd 2: P3, k5.
Rnd 3: P4, k4.
Rnd 4: P5, k3.
Rnd 5: P6, k2.
Rnd 6: P5, k3.
Rnd 7: P4, k4.
Rnd 8: P3, k5.
Rep Rnds 1-8 for patt.

PATTERN

Round Toe

Using a provisional cast on and leaving a tail of yarn at least 4"/10 cm long, CO 7 (8, 9, F) sts. Distribute sts among needles as you prefer, and join for working in the round. Knit 1 rnd.

Rnd 1: [K1, m1L] around. 14 (16, 18, F×2) sts.
Rnd 2: Knit.

Rnd 3: [K2, m1L] around. 21 (24, 27, F×3) sts.
Rnds 4–5: Knit.

Rnd 6: [K3, m1L] around. 28 (32, 36, F×4) sts.
Rnds 7–9: Knit.

Rnd 10: [K4, m1L] around. 35 (40, 45, F×5) sts.
Rnds 11–14: Knit.

Rnd 15: [K5, m1L] around. 42 (48, 54, F×6) sts.
Rnds 16–20: Knit.

Rnd 21: [K6, m1L] around. 49 (56, 63, F×7) sts.
Rnds 22–27: Knit.

Rnd 28: [K7, m1L] around. 56 (64, 72, S) sts.

Return to the provisional cast on, thread the yarn tail through the sts and pull tightly to close, then weave in the end.

Pm for beginning of rnd and another one halfway around the sock. The first half of the rnd is your instep, the second half is the sole of your sock.

The Rest of the Foot

For sizes Women's XS, Men's M/L and when F is an odd number:
Rnd 1: K2, work Mouchoir Stitch to 2 sts from marker, p2, knit to end of rnd.

All other sizes:
Rnd 1: Work Mouchoir Stitch to marker, knit to end of rnd.

The heel shaping takes 2½ (3, 3¼, X/11)"/ 6.5 (7.5, 8, X/4.4) cm or 28 (32, 36, X) rows, to work. Begin heel shaping when the foot of your sock is that much shorter than you want it to be.

WORKING OUT CUSTOM SIZING FOR MOUCHOIR, TOE UP

See page 49 for help with using this table. S must be divisible by 8.

Variable	How to calculate that variable	Write your result below
X	S/2	
A	(X / 2) – 3	
B	(X / 4) – 1	
C	(X / 2) – 1	
D	S + (X / 2)	
E	X – 4	
F	S / 8	

Gusset

For sizes Women's XS, Men's M/L and when F is an odd number:
Rnd 1: K2, work Mouchoir Stitch to 2 sts from marker, p2, sm, m1L, knit to end of rnd, m1R. 2 sts increased.
Rnd 2: Knit.

All other sizes:
Work Mouchoir Stitch to marker, sm, m1L, knit to end of rnd, m1R. 2 sts increased.
Rnd 2: Knit.

All sizes: Rep these 2 rnds 6 (7, 8, B) times more. 70 (80, 90, D) sts, total.

Heel Turn

Row 1 (RS): Continue in established patt to marker, remove it, k28 (32, 36, X), m1L. Turn.
Row 2 (WS): Sl1, p14 (16, 18, X/2), m1pR. Turn.

Row 3: Sl1, k13 (15, 17, C), m1L. Turn.

Row 4: Sl1, p12 (14, 16, C–1), m1pR. Turn.

Continue back and forth as established, working 1 less stitch before the increase in each row, until you have worked 13 (15, 17, C) rows total.

Last row (WS): Sl1, p2, m1pR. Turn. 56 (64, 72, S) heel sts.

Heel Flap

Set-up Row 1 (RS): Sl1, k14 (16, 18, X/2), ssk. Turn.
Set-up Row 2 (WS): Sl1, p26 (30, 34, X–2), p2tog. Turn.

Row 1: [Sl1, k1] 13 (15, 17, C) times, sl1, ssk. Turn.
Row 2: Sl1, p26 (30, 34, X–2), p2tog. Turn.
Rep these 2 rows until the heel has the same number of sts as the instep, and the total number of sts is the same as for the foot; 56 (64, 72, S) sts total.

Leg and Bind Off

For sizes Women's XS, Men's M/L and when F is an odd number:
Remove marker for start of rnd, k2, replace marker. This is the new start of the rnd.

All sizes:
Work Mouchoir Stitch 7 (8, 9, F) times around until leg is 2"/5 cm less than desired length.

Work [p1, k1] ribbing for 2"/5 cm.

BO. I like Jeny's Surprisingly Stretchy Bind Off, but any bind off that is stretchy enough for the sock to get over the foot will work. See page 47 for more information about bind offs for toe-up socks.

Finishing

Weave in all ends and block gently.

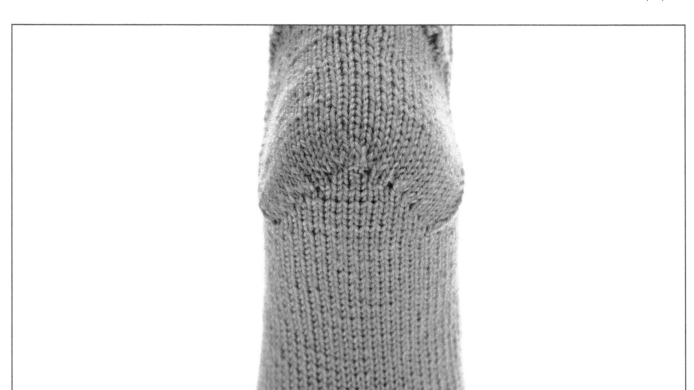

Checked & Square, Top Down

SIZES

Women's XS (Women's S, Women's M/
Men's S, Women's L/Men's M, Men's
L, Adjustable Size); shown in size
Women's M, Women's L and Child's 7.

FINISHED MEASUREMENTS

Foot circumference: 7 (7½, 8, 8½, 9½,
U)"/18 (19, 20.5, 21.5, 24, U) cm

Finished leg length: adjustable to fit
Finished foot length: adjustable to fit

MATERIALS

Simply Socks Yarn Company Simply
Sock Yarn (80% superwash wool, 20%
nylon; 175 yds/160m per 50g skein);
color: #260 Adobe, #830 Mocha, or
#620 Cerulean; 2 (2, 2, 2, 3, U) skeins

US#1 (2.25 mm) needles or size
needed to achieve gauge

3 stitch markers
Yarn needle

GAUGE

32 sts and 44 rnds = 4"/10 cm in both
stockinette stitch and patt stitch

SPECIAL STITCHES

Two-Stitch Check

(Worked over a multiple of 4 sts in the
round)
Rnds 1 and 2: [K2, p2] around.
Rnds 3 and 4: [P2, k2] around.

PATTERN

To work out your own custom sizing to
use in the instructions that follow, see
page 68.

Cast On and Leg

CO 56 (60, 64, 68, 76, S) sts. Distribute
sts among your needles as you prefer,
and join without twisting to work in
the round.

Work in [k2, p2] ribbing for 2"/5 cm.

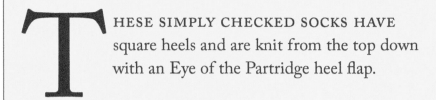

THESE SIMPLY CHECKED SOCKS HAVE
square heels and are knit from the top down
with an Eye of the Partridge heel flap.

Work Two-Stitch Check in the round,
repeating Rnds 1-4 until the leg measures 2½ (2¾, 3, 3, 3½, X/11)"/6.5 (7,
7.5, 8, 8.5, X/4.4) cm less than desired
length to bottom of heel, ending after
a Rnd 4.

Heel Flap

For sizes Women's XS and Women's
M/Men's S and when X/4 is a whole
number, you will need to shift the
stitches slightly. To do so, simply work
a k1. The next stitch is now the beginning of the row/round.

All sizes:
For the heel flap, you will work back
and forth over only the first half of
your stitches: 28 (30, 32, 34, 38, X) sts.
Leave the others on hold.

Eye of the Partridge stitch:
Row 1 (RS): [Sl1, k1] to end of heel
sts.
Rows 2 and 4 (WS): Sl1, purl to end.

WORKING OUT CUSTOM SIZING FOR CHECKED AND SQUARE, TOP DOWN

See page 49 for help with using this table. S must be divisible by 4.

Variable	How to calculate that variable	Write your result below
X	S/2	
A	$(X / 4) - 2$	
B	$(X - 4) / 4$ Round B down if it isn't whole.	
C	Take X and divide it by 3. This will rarely be even. The goal is to make the two outside edges with the same number of stitches, and let the center of the heel fall where it may. For our example socks, our heel flap is 32 stitches wide, so I would divide it as 11, 10, 11. The central stitches will form the strap running from the back of the heel to the bottom of the foot. You can adjust the size of the strap to your taste. If you do adjust the width of the strap, you will have to change the length, too, so take that into consideration. A wider strap makes a heel that takes fewer rows to work and will need more gusset stitches for the sock. A more narrow strap will take more rows to work and create a sock with a smaller gusset section. Let's call the center of heel (approx. X/3) C.	
E	Then E can be the outside edges on either side of C. Adjust things as much as you like, but $(2 \times E) + C$ must equal X.	
F	$(C / 4) - 1$	
H	$(X - 2) / 4$	
I	$S \times 0.6$	
J	$S \times 0.2$	
K	$S \times 0.3$	

The length of your sock toe will depend on which shape of toe you want:

- A short wide toe will be about $0.275 \times S$ rounds long.
- A medium wide toe will be about $0.325 \times S$ rounds long.
- A long wide toe will be about $0.45 \times S$ rounds long.

Take the length of the toe you want, in rounds, then divide that by your round gauge to get the approximate final length of your toe shaping.

Row 3: Sl1, k2, sl1, [k1, sl1] to 2 sts from end, k2.
Rep these 4 rows 5 (5, 6, 6, 7, A) more times.

For sizes Women's XS and Women's M/ Men's S and when A is a whole number: Work Rows 1–3 once more.

All other sizes: Work Rows 1–4 once more, then rep Row 1 once.

All sizes:
Next row (WS): Sl1, p9 (10, 11, 12, 13, E), pm, p8 (8, 8, 8,10, C–2), pm, p10 (11, 12, 13, 14, E + 1).

Heel Turn

Row 1 (RS): Sl1, knit to second marker, sm, ssk. Turn.
Row 2 (WS): Sl1, purl to second marker, sm, p2tog. Turn.
Rep these 2 rows 8 (9, 10, 11, 12, E–1) more times. 10 (10, 10, 10, 12, C) sts rem on heel. K5 (5, 5, 5, 6, C/2), pm for the start of the rnd.

Gusset

For sizes Women's XS and Women's M/ Men's S and when X/4 is a whole number:

Knit across rem heel sts, pick up and knit 1 stitch through each slipped-stitch chain on the edge of the heel flap, pm for start of instep; k1, p2, [k2, p2] 6 (–, 7, –, –, B) times, k1, pm for end of instep, pick up and knit sts for the left side of the gusset in the same way as you did for the right, knit to end of rnd. 66 (–, 74, –, –, S+C) sts on the needles.

Rnd 1: Knit to 2 sts before instep, k2tog, k1, [p2, k2] to 3 sts from marker, p2, k1, ssk, knit to end of rnd. 2 sts decreased.

Rnd 2: Knit to instep, sm, p1, [k2, p2] to 3 sts from marker, k2, p1, sm, knit to end of rnd.

Rnd 3: Knit to 2 sts before instep, k2tog, p1, [k2, p2] to 3 sts from marker, k2, p1, ssk, knit to end of rnd. 2 sts decreased.

Above: Women's Large, in Mocha; below: Child's size 7, in Cerulean

Rnd 4: Knit to instep, sm, k1, [p2, k2] to 3 sts from marker, p2, k1, sm, knit to end of rnd.

All other sizes:
Knit across rem heel sts, pick up and knit 1 stitch through each slipped-stitch chain on the edge of the heel flap, pm for start of instep; [p2, k2] – (7, –, 8, 9, H) times, k2, pm for end of instep, pick up and knit sts for the left side of the gusset in the same way as you did for the right, knit to end of rnd. – (70, –, 78, 88, S + C) sts on the needles.

Rnd 1: Knit to 2 sts before the instep, k2tog, [p2, k2] to 2 sts from marker, p2, ssk, knit to end of rnd. 2 sts decreased.

Rnd 2: Knit to instep, sm, [k2, p2] to 2 sts from marker, knit to end of rnd.

Rnd 3: Knit to 2 sts before the instep, k2tog, [k2, p2] to 2 sts from marker, k2, ssk, knit to end of rnd. 2 sts decreased.

Rnd 4: Knit to instep, sm, [p2, k2] to 2 sts from marker, p2, sm, knit to end of rnd.

All sizes:
Rep the 4 gusset shaping rows 1 (1, 1, 1, 2, F) more time(s), then work Rnds 1 and 2 only 1 (1, 1, 1, 0, –) more time(s). (When F is a whole number, end with Rnd 4; when F ends in 0.5, end with Rnd 2.) The sock should now have the same number of sts as it had on the leg: 56 (60, 64, 68, 76, S).

The Rest of the Foot

Once the gusset decreases are finished, leave stitch markers in place and work even in patt as follows, starting with Rnd 3 (3, 3, 3, 1, next consecutive rnd):

For sizes Women's XS and Women's M/ Men's S and when X/4 is a whole number:
Rnds 1 and 4: Knit to instep, k1, [p2, k2] to 3 sts from marker, p2, k1, knit to end of rnd.
Rnds 2 and 3: Knit to instep, p1, [k2, p2] to 3 sts from marker, k2, p1, knit to end of rnd.

All other sizes:
Rnds 1 and 4: Knit to instep, [p2, k2] to 2 sts from marker, p2, knit to end of rnd.
Rnds 2 and 3: Knit to instep, [k2, p2] to 2 sts from marker, knit to end of rnd.

Rep these 4 rnds until the foot of the sock is as long as you want, less the length needed for the toe, as follows:

If you are working the Short Wedge Toe, start toe shaping when your sock is 1½ (1½, 1¾, 1¾, 2, U)"/3.5 (4, 4, 4.5, 5, U) cm or 16 (17, 18, 19, 22, 0.275 × S) rnds shorter than the desired length of the sock.

If you are working the Medium Wedge Toe, start toe shaping when your sock is 1¾ (1¾, 2, 2, 2¼, U)"/4 (4.5, 5, 5, 5.5, U) cm or 18 (19, 21, 22, 24, 0.325 × S) rnds shorter than the desired length of the sock.

If you are working the Long Wedge Toe, start toe shaping when your sock is 2¼ (2¼, 2¾, 2¾, 3, U)"/5.5 (6, 6.5, 7, 7.5, U) or 25 (26, 29, 30, 33, 0.45 × S) rnds shorter than the desired length of the sock.

Toe

The pattern stitch ends here. The toe is worked in stockinette stitch.

SHORT WEDGE TOE

Rnd 1: *Knit to 2 sts before marker, k2tog, sm, ssk; rep from * once, knit to end of rnd. 4 sts decreased.
Rnd 2: Knit.

Rep Rnds 1 and 2 until you have 32 (36, 36, 40, 44, ~I) sts on the needles.

Then, rep only Rnd 1 until you have 16 (16, 20, 20, 20, ~K) sts on the needles. Knit to marker, graft rem sts closed.

MEDIUM WEDGE TOE

Rnd 1: *Knit to 2 sts before marker, k2tog, sm, ssk; rep from * once, knit to end of rnd. 4 sts decreased.
Rnd 2: Knit.

Rep Rnds 1 and 2 until you have 28 (32, 32, 36, 40, ~X) sts on the needles.

Then, rep only Rnd 1 until you have 12 (12, 12, 12, 16, ~J) sts on the needles. Knit to marker, graft rem sts closed.

LONG WEDGE TOE

Rnd 1: *Knit to 2 sts before marker, k2tog, sm, ssk; rep from * once, knit to end of rnd.
Rnds 2 and 3: Knit.

Rep Rnds 1–3 until you have 28 (32, 32, 36, 40, ~X) sts on the needles.

Then, rep only Rnd 1 until you have 12 (12, 12, 12, 16, ~J) sts on the needles. Knit to marker, graft rem sts closed.

Finishing

Weave in all ends and block gently.

Checked & Square, Toe Up

SIZES

Women's XS (Women's S, Women's M/ Men's S, Women's L/Men's M, Men's L, Adjustable Size); shown in size Women's M

FINISHED MEASUREMENTS

Foot circumference: 7 (7½, 8, 8½, 9½, U)"/18 (19, 20.5, 21.5, 24, U) cm

Finished leg length: adjustable to fit
Finished foot length: adjustable to fit

MATERIALS

Simply Socks Yarn Company Simply Sock Yarn (80% superwash wool, 20% nylon; 175 yds/160m per 50g skein); color: #876 Gray; 2 (2, 2, 2, 3, U) skeins

US#1 (2.25 mm) needles or size needed to achieve gauge

3 stitch markers
Yarn needle

If you are using a set of 5 dpns, 2 more could keep you from having to rearrange stitches.

I like to have a smaller, sharper needle at hand for working my lifted increases. It greatly reduces the stress on the yarn and my hands.

GAUGE

32 sts and 44 rnds = 4"/10 cm in both stockinette stitch and patt stitch

SPECIAL STITCHES

Two-Stitch Check

(Worked in the round over a multiple of 4 sts)
Rnds 1 and 2: [K2, p2] around.
Rnds 3 and 4: [P2, k2] around.

Two-Stitch Check, Split

(Worked in the round over a multiple of 4 sts, plus 4)
Rnds 1 and 2: K1, [p2, k2] to last 3 sts, p2, k1.

Rnds 3 and 4: P1, [k2, p2] to last 3 sts, k2, p1.

Two-Stitch Check, Balanced

(Worked in the round over a multiple of 4 sts, plus 2)
Rnds 1 and 2: [P2, k2] to 2 sts from the end, p2.
Rnds 3 and 4: [K2, p2] to 2 sts from the end, k2.

PATTERN

To work out your own custom sizing to use in the instructions that follow, see page 74.

Cast On and Toe

Choose the shape of toe you want to use. If you don't have a favorite, see page 38 for tips.

SHORT WEDGE TOE

CO 16 (20, 20, 20, 20, K) sts, using Judy's Magic Cast On. Knit 1 rnd, placing a marker for beginning of rnd and another one halfway around your toe.

Rnd 1: K1, m1L, knit to 1 st before marker, m1R, k1, sm, k1, m1L, knit to 1 st before end of rnd, m1R, k1. 4 sts increased.
Rep this rnd until you have 32 (36, 36, 40, 44, I) sts on the needles.

Rnd 1: K1, m1L, knit to 1 st before marker, m1R, k1, sm, k1, m1L, knit to 1 st before end of rnd, m1R, k1. 4 sts increased.
Rnd 2: Knit.
Rep these 2 rnds until you have 56 (60, 64, 68, 76, S) sts on the needles.

MEDIUM WEDGE TOE

CO 12 (12, 12, 16, 16, J) sts, using Judy's Magic Cast On. Knit 1 rnd, placing a marker for beginning of rnd and another one halfway around your toe.

Rnd 1: K1, m1L, knit to 1 st before marker, m1R, k1, sm, k1, m1L, knit to 1 st before end of rnd, m1R, k1. 4 sts increased.
Rep this rnd until you have 28 (32, 32, 36, 40, X) sts on the needles.

Rnd 1: K1, m1L, knit to 1 st before marker, m1R, k1, sm, k1, m1L, knit to 1 st before end of rnd, m1R, k1. 4 sts increased.
Rnd 2: Knit.
Rep these 2 rnds until you have 56 (60, 64, 68, 76, S) sts on the needles.

LONG WEDGE TOE

CO 12 (12, 12, 16, 16, J) sts, using Judy's Magic Cast On. Knit 1 rnd, placing a marker for beginning of rnd and another one halfway around your toe.

Rnd 1: K1, m1L, knit to 1 st before-marker, m1R, k1, sm, k1, m1L, knit to 1 st before end of rnd, m1R, k1. 4 sts increased.
Rep this rnd until you have 28 (32, 32, 36, 40, ~X) sts on the needles.

Rnd 1: K1, m1L, knit to 1 st before marker, m1R, k1, sm, k1, m1L, knit to 1 st before end of rnd, m1R, k1. 4 sts increased.
Rnds 2 and 3: Knit.
Rep these 3 rnds until you have 56 (60, 64, 68, 76, S) sts on the needles.

All styles should now have 28 (30, 32, 34, 38, X) sts each on instep and sole.

The Rest of the Foot

Leave the markers in place, and continue:

For sizes Women's XS and Women's M/ Men's S and when X/4 is a whole number:
Work Two-Stitch Check, Split on the instep sts, knit to end of rnd.

All other sizes:
Work Two-Stitch Check, Balanced on the instep sts, knit to end of rnd.

WORKING OUT CUSTOM SIZING FOR CHECKED AND SQUARE, TOE UP

See page 49 for help with using this table. S must be divisible by 4.

Variable	How to calculate that variable	Write your result below
X	S/2	
A	$(X / 4) - 2$	
B	$X / 2$	
C	Take X and divide it by 3. This will rarely be even. The goal is to make the two outside edges with the same number of stitches, and let the center of the heel fall where it may. For our example socks, our heel flap is 32 stitches wide, so I would divide it as 11, 10, 11. The central stitches will form the strap running from the back of the heel to the bottom of the foot. You can adjust the size of the strap to your taste. If you do adjust the width of the strap, you will have to change the length, too, so take that into consideration. A wider strap makes a heel that takes fewer rows to work and will need more gusset stitches for the sock. A more narrow strap will take more rows to work and create a sock with a smaller gusset section. Let's call the center of heel C (approx. $X / 3$).	
E	Then E can be the outside edges on either side of C. Adjust things as much as you like, but $(2 \times E) + C$ must equal X.	
I	$S \times 0.6$ Round to multiple of 4.	
J	$S \times 0.2$ Round to multiple of 4.	
K	$S \times 0.3$ Round to multiple of 4.	
L	$(S + C) - (S / 4)$	
M	$(X - 6) / 2$	
N	$(X - 2) / 2$	

All sizes:
Rep patt Rnds 1-4 until the foot of the sock is as long as you want, less the length needed for the gusset and heel shaping: 2½ (2¾, 3, 3, 3½, X/11)"/ 6.5 (7, 7.5, 8, 8.5, X/4.4) cm or 28 (30, 32, 34, 38, X) rnds.

Gusset

Rnd 1: Work Two-Stitch Check as established, sm, m1L, knit to end of rnd, m1R. 2 sts increased.

Rnd 2: Work Two-Stitch Check as established, sm, knit to end of rnd. Rep these 2 rnds until you have added 10 (10, 10, 10, 12, C) sts total. 66 (70, 74, 78, 88, S+C) sts.

Heel Turn

Set-up Row: Work in patt across instep, remove marker, then knit across heel until 14 (15, 16, 17, 19, B) sts remain. 52 (55, 58, 61, 69, L) sts worked. Turn.

You will continue over just the 10 (10, 10, 10, 12, C) center sts of the sole; these are the heel strap sts. (This is where some spare needles might come in handy.)

Row 1 (WS): Sl1, p9 (9, 9, 9, 11, C−1). Turn.
Row 2 (RS): Sl1, k9 (9, 9, 9, 11, C−1). Turn.
Rep these 2 rows 8 (9, 10, 11, 12, E−1) more times; 18 (20, 22, 24, 26, 2 × E) rows worked in total.

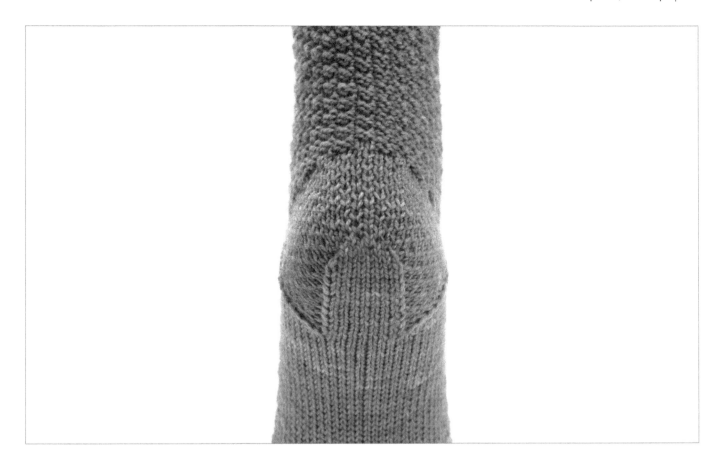

Pick up and knit all but 1 slipped stitch from along the edge of the piece you just made, pm for heel flap, pick up that last stitch. Knit rem heel sts, work in patt across the instep sts, then knit around to the other side of the heel strap. Pick up and knit 1 stitch from the heel strap, place another heel flap marker, then pick up and knit the rest of your slipped edge sts. 84 (90, 96, 102, 114, S+X) sts.

Heel Flap

Set-up Row 1 (RS): Knit to marker, sm, ssk. Turn.
Set-up Row 2 (WS): Sl1, purl to second marker, sm, p2tog. Turn.

Row 1 (RS): Sl1, k2, [sl1, k1] 11 (12, 13, 14, 16, M) times, k2, sm, ssk. Turn.
Rows 2 and 4 (WS): Sl1, purl to second marker, sm, p2tog. Turn.

Row 3: [Sl1, k1] 13 (14, 15, 16, 18, N) times, sl1, sm, ssk. Turn.
Rep these 4 rows 5 (5, 6, 6, 7, A) more times.

For sizes Women's XS and Women's M/ Men's S and when A is a whole number: Work Rows 1-2 once more.

All other sizes: Work Rows 1-4 once more.

You should now have 56 (60, 64, 68, 76, S) sts on the needles.

Knit to beginning of rnd, removing heel flap markers.

Leg and Bind Off

For sizes Women's XS and Women's M/ Men's S and when X/4 is a whole number: You will need to shift the stitches slightly to work the leg in patt. To do

this, remove the marker, work the next stitch in patt, and replace the marker for the new beginning of rnd.

All sizes:
Keeping the patt as established on the instep, work all sts in Two-Stitch Check until leg is 2"/5 cm less than the desired length, ending after a patt Rnd 2 or 4.

Work in [k2, p2] ribbing for 2"/5 cm.

BO. I like Jeny's Surprisingly Stretchy Bind Off, but any bind off that is stretchy enough for the sock to get over the foot will work. Please see page 47 for more information about bind offs for toe-up socks.

Finishing

Weave in all ends and block gently.

Bootstrap

Sizes

Women's XS (Women's S, Women's M/ Men's S, Women's L/Men's M, Men's L, Adjustable Size); shown in size Women's M

Finished Measurements

Foot circumference: 7 (7½, 8, 8½, 9½, U)"/18 (19, 20.5, 21.5, 24, U) cm

Finished leg length: adjustable to fit
Finished foot length: adjustable to fit

Materials

Simply Socks Yarn Company Simply Sock Yarn (80% superwash wool, 20% nylon; 175 yds/160m per 50g skein); color: #830 Mocha; 2 (2, 2, 2, 3, U) skeins

US#1 (2.25 mm) needles or size needed to achieve gauge

5 stitch markers
Yarn needle

Gauge

32 sts and 44 rnds = 4"/10 cm in stockinette stitch

Pattern

To work out your own custom sizing to use in the instructions that follow, see page 78.

Cast On and Leg

CO 56 (60, 64, 68, 76, S) sts. Distribute sts among your needles as you prefer, and join without twisting to work in the round.

Work in [k1, p1] ribbing for 2"/5 cm.

Set-up Rnd: K2, pm, k21 (22, 24, 26, 29, Z), pm, knit to end.

Rnd 1: *Knit to marker, p3 (4, 4, 4, 5, A); rep from * once, knit to end.
Rnd 2: Knit.

THESE BOOTSTRAP SOCKS HAVE A simple line of garter-stitch running down both sides of the leg that continues onto the heel. In my mind at least, they slightly mimic the most fun detail on a western-style boot—that little seam running down the outside of the leg. The sock ends with a wide toe that can be made short, medium or long.

Besides just looking cool, that little line of garter stitch seems to make the knitting go faster than plain stockinette. As a bonus, it makes counting rounds absurdly easy, so you don't have to worry about losing your place when you make the second sock (or the heel flap).

For more information on the Balbriggan heel used in this sock, see page 27.

Rep these 2 rnds until the leg is 2 (2¼, 2¼, 2½, 2¾, B/11)"/5 (5.5, 6, 6.5, 7, B/4.4) cm less than desired length to bottom of heel.

Heel Flap

For the heel flap, you will work back and forth over only the first half of your sts: 28 (30, 32, 34, 38, X) sts. Leave the others on hold.

Row 1 (RS): Sl1, *knit to marker, p3 (4, 4, 4, 5, A); rep from * once, k2. Turn.
Row 2 (WS): Sl1, purl to end.
Rep these 2 rows 10 (11, 12, 13, 14, C) more times.

Heel Turn

Remove the pattern markers. The garter-stitch stripe ends now.

Set-up Row 1 (RS): Sl1, k4 (5, 5, 5, 6, Y-1), pm, ssk, k5 (5, 6, 7, 8, H), k2tog, pm, ssk, k5 (5, 6, 7, 8, H), k2tog, pm, knit to end. 24 (26, 28, 30, 34, X–4) sts on the needles.
Set-up Row 2 (WS): Sl1, purl to end.

Row 1 (RS): Sl1, knit to marker, sm, ssk, knit to 2 sts before marker, k2tog, sm, ssk, knit to 2 sts before marker, k2tog, sm, knit to end. 4 sts decreased.
Row 2 (WS): Sl1, purl to end.

If necessary, rep these 2 rows until you have 5 (5, 4, 5, 4, U) sts between your first and second markers (and second and third markers). 20 (22, 20, 22, 22, U) sts on the needles. Work one more RS row then work the WS row to the second marker. 16 (18, 16, 18, 18, U) sts on the needles.

Break the yarn, leaving a long tail. Fold the work so that the wrong sides of the heel flap are together. Using a darning needle, graft rem heel sts together.

Note: You may be tempted to use the tail left over from grafting to pick up some stitches, then join new yarn. I don't like to do this because I find that the area right at the end of the join has a tendency to look messy. I prefer to save that little tail to darn in and help firm up that area.

WORKING OUT CUSTOM SIZING FOR BOOTSTRAP

See page 49 for help with using this table. S must be divisible by 2.

Variable	How to calculate that variable	Write your result below
X	S/2	
Y	X / 5 Round this down to the nearest whole number.	
A	Y – 2 This is the width of the garter-stitch "bootstrap."	
Z	X – Y – 2	
B	X × 0.8 Round this to the nearest even number.	
C	(B / 2) – 1	
D	S × 0.6	
E	S × 0.2	
F	S × 0.3	
H	(X / 2) – Y – 4	

The length of your sock toe will depend on which shape of toe you want.

- A short wide toe will be about 0.275 × S rounds long.

- A medium wide toe will be about 0.325 × S rounds long.

- A long wide toe will be about 0.45 × S rounds long.

Take the length of the toe you want, in rounds, then divide that by your round gauge to get the approximate final length of your toe shaping.

IF X IS AN EVEN NUMBER:

Place markers at Y sts from the beginning of the row, X/2 sts and Y sts from the end of the row.

Row 1 (RS): Sl1, knit to marker, sm, ssk, knit to 2 sts before marker, k2tog, sm, ssk, knit to 2 sts before marker, k2tog, sm, knit to end. 4 sts decreased.
Row 2 (WS): Sl1, purl to end.

Rep these 2 rows until you have 4 or 5 sts between your first and second marker. Work 1 more RS row and work the WS row to the second marker.

IF X IS AN ODD NUMBER, ROUND X/2 DOWN TO THE NEAREST WHOLE NUMBER:

Place markers at Y sts from the beginning of the row, X/2 sts and Y sts from the end of the row.

Row 1 (RS): Sl1, knit to marker, sm, ssk, knit to 2 sts before marker, k2tog, sm, k1, ssk, knit to 2 sts before marker, k2tog, sm, knit to end. 4 sts decreased.
Row 2 (WS): Sl1, purl to end.

Rep these 2 rows until you have 4 or 5 sts between your first and second marker. Work 1 more RS row and work the WS row until 2 sts from the second marker, p2tog.

Gusset

Rejoin yarn at the center of the heel. Create stitches for the right side of the sole and gusset by picking up and knitting 14 (15, 17, 18, 20, U) sts (1 stitch through each slipped-stitch chain on the edge of the heel flap) pm for start of instep, knit across instep, place a second marker for end of instep. Create sts for the left side of the sole and gusset by picking up and knitting 14 (15, 17, 18, 20, U) sts (1 stitch through each slipped-stitch chain on the edge of the heel flap). 56 (60, 66, 70, 78, S+2) sts on the needles.

Gusset Decreases

XS and S only: skip to The Rest of the Foot.

Rnd 1: Knit to 2 sts before the instep marker, k2tog, knit to marker, ssk, knit to end of rnd. 2 sts decreased.
Rnd 2: Knit.

The sock should now have the same number of sts as it had on the leg. 56 (60, 64, 68, 76, S) sts.

The Rest of the Foot

Leave the stitch markers in place, and continue:

Work in stockinette stitch until the foot of the sock is as long as you want, less the length needed for the toe, as follows:

If you are working the Short Wide Toe, start toe shaping when your sock is 1½ (1½, 1¾, 1¾, 2, U)"/3.5 (4, 4, 4.5, 5, U) cm or 16 (17, 18, 19, 22, 0.275 × S) rnds shorter than the desired length of the sock.

If you are working the Medium Wide Toe, start toe shaping when your sock is 1¾ (1¾, 2, 2, 2¼, U)"/4 (4.5, 5, 5, 5.5, U) cm or 18 (19, 21, 22, 24, 0.325 × S) rnds shorter than the desired length of the sock.

If you are working the Long Wide Toe, start toe shaping when your sock is 2¼ (2¼, 2¾, 2¾, 3, U)"/5.5 (6, 6.5, 7, 7.5,

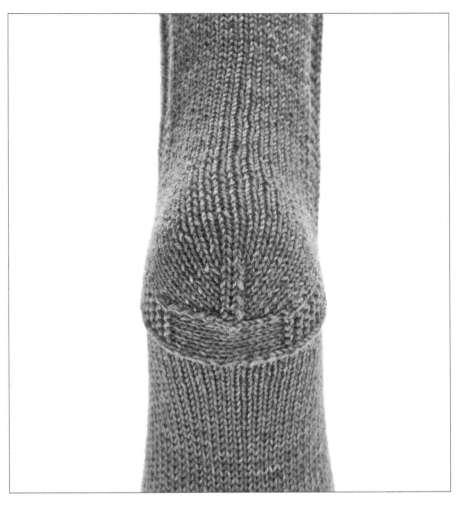

U) cm or 25 (26, 29, 30, 33, 0.45 × S) rnds shorter than the desired length of the sock.

Toe

SHORT WIDE TOE

Rnd 1: *Knit to 3 sts before marker, k2tog, k2, ssk; rep from * once, knit to end of rnd. 4 sts decreased.
Rnd 2: Knit.

Rep Rnds 1 and 2 until you have 32 (36, 36, 40, 44, ~D) sts on the needles. Then, rep only Rnd 1 until you have 16 (16, 20, 20, 20, ~F) sts on the needles. Knit to marker, graft rem sts closed.

MEDIUM WIDE TOE

Rnd 1: *Knit to 3 sts before marker, k2tog, k2, ssk; rep from * once, knit to end of rnd. 4 sts decreased.
Rnd 2: Knit.

Rep Rnds 1 and 2 until you have 28 (32, 32, 36, 40, ~X) sts on the needles.
Then, rep only Rnd 1 until you have 12 (12, 12, 12, 16, ~E) sts on the needles. Knit to marker, graft rem sts closed.

LONG WIDE TOE

Rnd 1: *Knit to 3 sts before marker, k2tog, k2, ssk; rep from * once, knit to end of rnd. 4 sts decreased.
Rnds 2 and 3: Knit.

Rep Rnds 1–3 until you have 28 (32, 32, 36, 40, ~X) sts on the needles. Then, rep only Rnd 1 until you have 12 (12, 12, 12, 16, ~E) sts on the needles. Knit to marker, graft rem sts closed.

Finishing

Weave in all ends and block gently.

Uncommon Dragon

SIZES

Women's XS (Women's S, Women's M/
Men's S, Women's L/Men's M, Men's
L); shown in size Women's M

FINISHED MEASUREMENTS

Foot circumference: 7 (7½, 8, 8½,
9½)"/18 (19, 20.5, 21.5, 24) cm

Finished leg length: adjustable to fit
Finished foot length: adjustable to fit

MATERIALS

Simply Socks Yarn Company Simply
Sock Yarn (80% superwash wool, 20%
nylon; 175 yds/160m per 50g skein);
color: #530 Wasabi or #410 Golden;
2 (2, 2, 2, 3) skeins

US#1 (2.25 mm) needles or size
needed to achieve gauge

4 stitch markers
Yarn needle

I like to have a smaller, sharper needle
at hand for working my lifted increases.
It greatly reduces the stress on the yarn
and my hands.

GAUGE

32 sts and 44 rnds = 4"/10 cm in stockinette stitch

36 sts and 46 rnds = 4"/10 cm in Little
Dragon stitch

PATTERN NOTES

There are two versions of the stitch
pattern for these socks, Little Dragon
Stitch and Extended Little Dragon
Stitch. This is to accommodate the
smaller number of stitches for the
smaller sizes of the socks. Work from
written or charted instructions as you
prefer.

THESE SOCKS USE A VARIATION ON ONE OF my very favorite stitch patterns—I call it Little Dragon Stitch. The stitch pattern is pretty, but quite a bit wider than some of the other ones out there, so there is no completely adjustable size for this pattern. To help manage sizing with such a wide stitch pattern, I added ribbing to the sides of the legs of most sizes. It also features a Shaped Common Heel, which needs to be grafted closed, but has no short rows to work.

In photography, we sometimes tell models that a position that feels silly is the one that looks great. This heel is kind of the other way around. It looks rather terrible, especially when freshly worked and unblocked, but it wears like an absolute dream, and is wonderfully suited to people with wide feet and heels.

Through a bit of sneakiness, I managed to carry Little Dragon a little further than usual—down the back of the heel. That sneakiness means that I haven't written this pattern in a plug-in-your-own numbers way, but there is a good range of sizes. It may disconcert some knitters that the front and back of the leg of the sock, for most sizes, are slightly different from one another. I've sacrificed perfect symmetry there to allow the heel flap to flow beautifully from the leg.

There is a very small gusset for this heel, and gusset increases are closer to the bottom of the sock than in many designs. I love the way it looks, and I hope you agree with me.

The stitch pattern would be rather uncomfortable for the bottom of a sock, so that part is in Stockinette stitch. The sole of the sock has fewer stitches than the top, to make up for their different stitch gauges.

The sock ends with what I call a Swirl toe. It's very easy to work and looks rather cool, if I do say so myself.

LITTLE DRAGON STITCH CHART

Note that charts do not show even-numbered rounds.

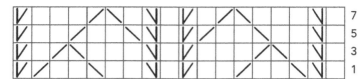

EXTENDED LITTLE DRAGON STITCH CHART

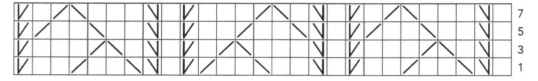

	knit
	m1L
	m1R
	k2tog
	ssk

SPECIAL STITCHES

Little Dragon Stitch (in the Round)

(Worked over 18 sts in the round)

Rnd 1: K1, m1L, ssk, k2, k2tog, k2, m1R, k1, m1L, k2, ssk, k2, k2tog, m1R.
Rnd 2 and all other even-numbered rnds: Knit.
Rnd 3: K1, m1L, k1, ssk, k2tog, k3, m1R, k1, m1L, k3, ssk, k2tog, k1, m1R.
Rnd 5: K1, m1L, k2, ssk, k2, k2tog, m1R, k1, m1L, ssk, k2, k2tog, k2, m1R.
Rnd 7: K1, m1L, k3, ssk, k2tog, kl, m1R, k1, m1L, k1, ssk, k2tog, k3, m1R.
Rnd 8: Knit.
Rep Rnds 1–8 for patt.

Little Dragon Stitch (Flat)

(Worked over 18 sts, flat)

Row 1 (RS): K1, m1L, ssk, k2, k2tog, k2, m1R, k1, m1L, k2, ssk, k2, k2tog, m1R.
Row 2 (WS) and all other even-numbered rows: Purl.
Row 3: K1, m1L, k1, ssk, k2tog, k3, m1R, k1, m1L, k3, ssk, k2tog, k1, m1R.
Row 5: K1, m1L, k2, ssk, k2, k2tog, m1R, k1, m1L, ssk, k2, k2tog, k2, m1R.
Row 7: K1, m1L, k3, ssk, k2tog, kl, m1R, k1, m1L, k1, ssk, k2tog, k3, m1R.
Row 8: Purl.
Rep Rows 1-8 for patt.

Extended Little Dragon Stitch (in the Round)

(Worked over 27 sts in the round)

Rnd 1: K1, m1L, ssk, k2, k2tog, k2, m1R, k1, m1L, k2, ssk, k2, k2tog, m1R, k1, m1L, ssk, k2, k2tog, k2, m1R.
Rnd 2 and all other even-numbered rnds: Knit.
Rnd 3: K1, m1L, k1, ssk, k2tog, k3, m1R, k1, m1L, k3, ssk, k2tog, k1, m1R, k1, m1L, k1, ssk, k2tog, k3, m1R.
Rnd 5: K1, m1L, k2, ssk, k2, k2tog, m1R, k1, m1L, ssk, k2, k2tog, k2, m1R, k1, m1L, k2, ssk, k2, k2tog, m1R.
Rnd 7: K1, m1L, k3, ssk, k2tog, kl, m1R, k1, m1L, k1, ssk, k2tog, k3, m1R, k1, m1L, k3, ssk, k2tog, kl, m1R.
Rnd 8: Knit.
Rep Rnds 1-8 for patt.

Extended Little Dragon Stitch (Flat)

(Worked over 27 sts, flat)

Row 1 (RS): K1, m1L, ssk, k2, k2tog, k2, m1R, k1, m1L, k2, ssk, k2, k2tog, m1R, k1, m1L, ssk, k2, k2tog, k2, m1R.
Row 2 (WS) and all other even-numbered rows: Purl.
Row 3: K1, m1L, k1, ssk, k2tog, k3, m1R, k1, m1L, k3, ssk, k2tog, k1, m1R, k1, m1L, k1, ssk, k2tog, k3, m1R.
Row 5: K1, m1L, k2, ssk, k2, k2tog, m1R, k1, m1L, ssk, k2, k2tog, k2, m1R, k1, m1L, k2, ssk, k2, k2tog, m1R.

Row 7: K1, m1L, k3, ssk, k2tog, kl, m1R, k1, m1L, k1, ssk, k2tog, k3, m1R, k1, m1L, k3, ssk, k2tog, kl, m1R.
Row 8: Purl.
Rep Rows 1-8 for patt.

PATTERN

Cast On and Leg

CO 64 (68, 72, 78, 86) sts. Distribute sts among your needles as you prefer, and join, being careful not to twist.

Work [k1, p1] ribbing for 2"/5 cm.

Pm halfway around, dividing first half of rnd (front of leg) from second half of rnd (back of leg).

Women's XS: P2, work Extended Little Dragon Stitch to 3 sts before marker, k1, p2, k2, work Extended Little Dragon Stitch to 3 sts before end of rnd, k3.

Women's S: K1, p2, work Extended Little Dragon Stitch to 4 sts before marker, k1, p2, k4, work Extended Little Dragon Stitch to 4 sts before end of rnd, k4.

Women's M/Men's S: Work Little Dragon Stitch around.

Women's L/Men's M: P1, work Little Dragon Stitch to 2 sts before marker, k1, p1, k1, work Little Dragon Stitch to 2 sts before end of rnd, k2.

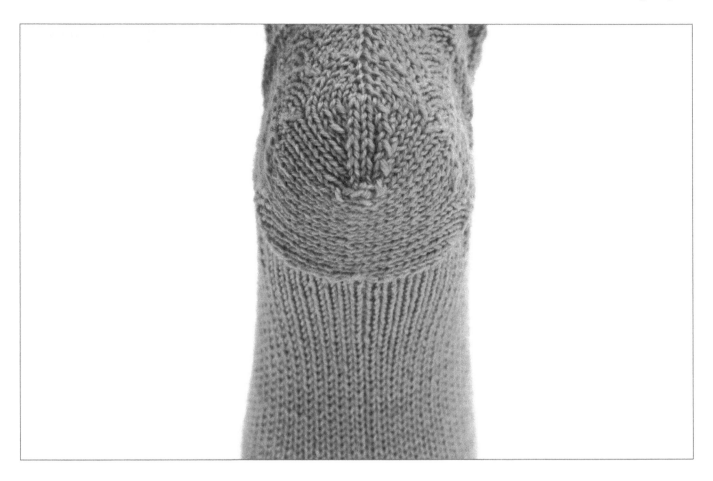

Men's L: K1, p2, work Little Dragon Stitch to 4 sts before marker, k1, p2, k4, work Little Dragon Stitch to 4 sts before end of rnd, k4.

Continue in patt until leg is as long as desired, less 2¼ (2½, 2½, 2¾, 3)"/5.5 (6, 6, 6.5, 7.5) cm.

SET-UP FOR HEEL FLAP:

Work in patt across front of leg to marker. Those 32 (34, 36, 39, 43) sts will now be put on hold as you work the heel. Make a note of which chart you worked and the last round you worked—you'll need this later when you resume the instep. The heel flap will be worked back and forth over the remaining 32 (34, 36, 39, 43) sts.

Heel Flap

Women's XS:
Row 1 (RS): Sl1, k1, work next row of Extended Little Dragon Stitch to 3 sts before end of row, k3.

Row 2 (WS): Sl1, purl to end.

Women's S:
Row 1 (RS): Sl1, k2, work next row of Extended Little Dragon Stitch to 4 sts before end of row, k4.
Row 2 (WS): Sl1, purl to end.

Women's M/Men's S:
Set-up Row 1 (RS): CO 1 st using Backwards Loop Cast On, work next row of Little Dragon Stitch across, CO 1 st. – (–, 38, –, –) sts.
Set-up Row 2 (WS): Sl1, purl to end.

Row 1: Sl1, work next row of Little Dragon Stitch to 1 st before end of row, k1.
Row 2: Sl1, purl to end.

Women's L/Men's M:
Row 1 (RS): Sl1, work next row of Little Dragon Stitch to 2 sts before end of row, k2.
Row 2 (WS): Sl1, purl to end.

Men's L:
Row 1 (RS): Sl1, k2, work next row of Little Dragon Stitch to 4 sts before end of row, k4.
Row 2 (WS): Sl1, purl to end.

All sizes: Rep these 2 rows 12 (13, 12, 14, 16) times more.

Heel Turn

Set-up Row 1 (RS): Sl1, k13 (14, 16, 16, 18), k2tog, pm, k0 (0, 0, 1, 1), ssk, knit to end of heel flap. 30 (32, 36, 37, 41) sts.
Set-up Row 2 (WS): Sl1, purl to end.

Row 1 (RS): Sl1, knit to 2 sts from marker, k2tog, k0 (0, 0, 1, 1), ssk, knit to end of heel flap. 2 sts decreased.
Row 2 (WS): Sl1, purl to end.

Rep these 2 rows 1 (1, 1, 2, 2) time(s) more, and then work Row 1 once more. 24 (26, 30, 29, 33) sts.

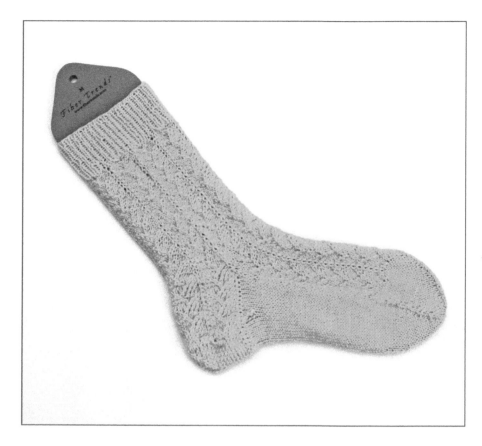

Final Heel Shaping Row (WS): Sl1, p11 (12, 14, 12, 14), p2tog 0 (0, 0, 1, 1) times. 24 (26, 30, 28, 32) sts.

Fold the work so that the WS faces are together, and graft the first half of the row to the second half of the row.

Gusset

Note: You may be tempted to use the tail left over from grafting to pick up some stitches, then join new yarn. I don't like to do this because I find that the area right at the end of the join has a tendency to look messy. So I prefer to use that little tail to darn in and help firm up that area.

Rejoin yarn where you left off: at the center bottom of the heel with RS facing. To create sts for the right half of the sole and gusset, pick up and knit 8 sts from along the edge of the piece you just grafted, pm, pick up and knit 10 (11, 12, 13, 15) sts from along the edge of the heel flap, then pm for start of instep. Continuing the patt stitch from where you left off, work across the 32 (34, 36, 39, 43) sts you left on hold for the instep, pm for end of instep. Create sts for the left half of the sole and gusset by picking up and knitting 10 (11, 12, 13, 15) sts from along the edge of the heel flap, pm, pick up and knit 8 more sts from along the edge of the piece you just grafted. 68 (72, 76, 81, 89) sts.

Rnd 1: Knit to marker, ssk, knit to instep marker, work in patt to end of instep, knit to 2 sts from marker, k2tog, knit to end. 2 sts decreased.
Rnd 2: Knit to instep marker, work in patt to end of instep, knit to end of rnd.

Rep these 2 rnds 3 times more. 60 (64, 68, 73, 81) sts total: 28 (30, 32, 34, 38) sts on the sole, and 32 (34, 36, 39, 43) sts on the instep.

The Rest of the Foot

Remove the markers that aren't for the start of the round or the instep and continue to rep only Rnd 2 until foot of sock is as long as you want, less 1¾ (2, 2, 2, 2½)"/4.5 (5, 5, 5, 5.5) cm or 20 (21, 22, 23, 25) rnds for the toe. Remove the marker at the end of the instep before beginning the toe.

A word of caution: My dragon stitch, when freshly worked and unblocked, tends to draw up a bit. When blocked, the heel flap on this sock should be approx 1¾ (2, 2, 2¼, 2½)"/4.5 (4.5, 5.5, 5.5, 6) cm wide, measured from the center-back of the heel to the outer edge of the heel flap. So, when measuring the sock length, make sure your heel stitches are flat.

I like this stitch pattern best when it ends with either a Rnd 3 or 7. If you reach this point but are not quite ready to make the toe, simply work in stockinette around until you get there. I had to do this for two rounds.

Toe

Set-up Rnd: [K15 (16, 18, 17, 20), pm] 3 times, knit to 0 (0, 0, 2, 2) sts from end of rnd, k2tog 0 (0, 0, 1, 1) times. 60 (64, 68, 72, 80) sts.

Rnd 1: [Knit to 2 sts before marker, k2tog, sm] 3 times, knit to 2 sts before end of rnd, k2tog. 4 sts decreased.
Rnd 2: Knit.

Rep these 2 rnds 5 times more. 36 (40, 44, 48, 56) sts.

Work Rnd 1 only until 8 sts rem. Break yarn, leaving a 6"/15cm tail. With a darning needle, thread the yarn through the remaining stitches. Go through twice, if you want the extra security. Pull stitches tightly, bring the yarn to the inside of the sock, and weave the tail in.

Finishing

Weave in all ends and block gently.

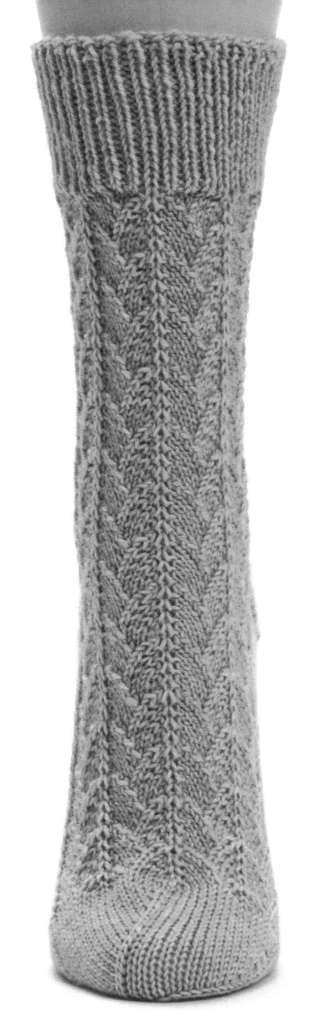

Dyad, Top Down

SIZES

Women's XS (Women's S, Women's M/
Men's S, Women's L/Men's M, Men's
L, Adjustable Size); shown in size
Women's M

FINISHED MEASUREMENTS

Foot circumference: 7 (7½, 8, 8½, 9½,
U)"/18 (19, 20.5, 21.5, 24, U) cm

Finished leg length: adjustable to fit

Finished foot length: adjustable to fit

MATERIALS

Simply Socks Yarn Company Simply
Sock Yarn (80% superwash wool, 20%
nylon; 175 yds/160m per 50g skein)

- [Color A] #830 Mocha; 2 skeins
- [Color B] #260 Adobe; 1 skein

US#1 (2.25 mm) needles or size
needed to achieve gauge

3 stitch markers
Yarn needle

GAUGE

32 sts and 44 rnds = 4"/10 cm in
stockinette stitch

PATTERN

To work out your own custom sizing to
use in the instructions that follow, see
page 88.

Cast On and Leg

Using color A, CO 56 (60, 64, 68,
76, S) sts. Distribute sts among your
needles as you prefer, and join without
twisting to work in the round.

Work [k1, p1] ribbing for 2"/5 cm.

Continue in stockinette stitch until the
leg is approx 2"/5 cm shorter than your
desired length to bottom of heel. Break
color A. Join color B.

I CHOSE "DYAD" AS THE NAME FOR THESE
socks as a kind of reference to my thought process.
I wanted to explore the easiest way I know to make
a two-color sock: one color for the heel and toe,
and another for the rest of the sock. I was also eager to use
a band heel and a toe to match.

So (in my mind), bands with two colors = two things to
do with musical bands = two notes = two notes played
together = (a short trip to Google) = dyad. Dyad also
means, in many other contexts, sets of two. What could be
more perfect for a pair of socks?

I hope you find harmony with these easy socks. The band
heel is an interesting exercise in shaping. The gusset
shaping happens almost entirely within the heel, leaving
the foot of the sock mostly undisturbed. A straight heel
flap gives way to a short area of shaping with decreases.
The lines created by the decreases are then continued with
back-and-forth shaping, which is what actually turns the
heel.

A sideways toe matches this heel quite nicely. It fits like a
wedge toe and can be made short, medium or long, to fit
wide, medium, or pointy toes.

Heel Shaping

With this heel your gusset shaping is
worked as you are turning the heel.
You will be able to just knit straight on
for the foot after picking up the gusset
stitches. It is worked in three parts.

For the heel flap, you will work back
and forth over only the first half of your
sts: 28 (30, 32, 34, 38, X) sts. Leave the
others on hold.

PART 1

Set-up Row 1 (RS): K28 (30, 32, 34,
38, X) sts. Turn.
Set-up Row 2 (WS): Sl1, purl to end.

Row 1 (RS): Sl1, knit to end.
Row 2 (WS): Sl1, purl to end.
Rep these 2 rows for the heel flap 6 (7,
8, 8, 9, F) more times.

PART 2

Set-up Row 1 (RS): K11 (12, 13, 14,
15, I), pm, k6 (6, 6, 6, 8, H), pm, k11
(12, 13, 14, 15, I).
Set-up Row 2 (WS): Sl1, purl to end
of row.

Row 1 (RS): Sl1, knit to 2 sts from
marker, k2tog, sm, knit to marker, ssk,
knit to end of row. 2 sts decreased.
Row 2: (WS): Sl1, purl to end of row.

WORKING OUT CUSTOM SIZING FOR DYAD, TOP DOWN

See page 49 for help with using this table. S must be divisible by 2.

Variable	How to calculate that variable	Write your result below
X	S/2	
A	X × 0.6 This is the number of heel flap rows you will work before adding shaping, so round this to a whole, even number.	
B	X / 4 These are the stitches you will have left over after heel shaping is finished. If X is odd, this needs to be odd. If X is even, this needs to be even.	
C	X / 10 This is the number of repeats in section 2. It needs to be a whole number, but it can be odd or even.	
Add up A, B and 2 × C. If this total is not larger than or equal to X, increase A until it is. If it is a little larger than X, you will need to work a small amount of gusset shaping after picking up gusset stitches.		
F	(A / 2) − 2	
H	(X / 4) − 2 Round to a whole number.	
I	(X − H) / 2	
J	(A / 2) + C	
K	X + (2 × J) + B	
L	(K − S) / 2	
Q	X − (2 × C) + 2	
D	For Short Toes: D = (S × 0.3) / 2 = the number of stitches you will have left over on the top and bottom of your toe when toe shaping is finished. This needs to be a whole, even number. For Medium and Long Toes: D = (S × 0.2) / 2 = the number of stitches you will have left over on the top and bottom of your toe when toe shaping is finished. This needs to be a whole, even number.	
E	(D / 2) − 1	
M	(D / 2) + 1	
N	D − 2	
P	S × 0.6	

The length of your sock toe will depend on which shape of toe you want.

- A short sideways toe will be about 0.275 × S rounds long.
- A medium sideways toe will be about 0.325 × S rounds long.
- A long sideways toe will be about 0.45 × S rounds long.

Take the length of the toe you want, in rounds, then divide that by your round gauge to get the approximate final length of your toe shaping.

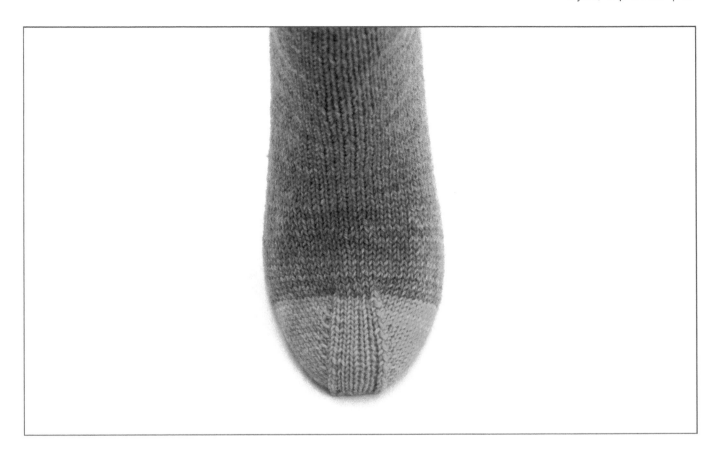

Rep these 2 rows 1 (1, 1, 1, 2, C–2) more times. 24 (26, 28, 30, 320, Q??) heel sts rem.

PART 3

Row 1 (RS): Sl1, knit to second marker, sm, ssk. Turn.
Row 2 (WS): Sl1, purl to second marker, sm, p2tog. Turn.
Rep these 2 rows until you have 8 (8, 8, 8, 10, B) sts left on the heel, stopping after a WS row.

Gusset

Break color B; join color A. K4 (4, 4, 4, 5, B/2), pm for the start of the rnd. Knit across the rem flap sts, then create the right side of the gusset by picking up and knitting 11 (12, 13, 13, 15, J) sts, one for each slipped-stitch chain on the edge of the heel flap; pm for start of instep, k28 (30, 32, 34, 38, X) sts across the instep, place a second marker for end of instep. Create the left side of the gusset by picking up and knitting

11 (12, 13, 13, 15, J) sts, one for each slipped-stitch chain on the edge of the heel flap; knit to end of rnd. 58 (62, 66, 68, 78, K) sts, total.

All sizes except Women's L/Men's M:
Rnd 1: Knit to 2 sts before the instep, k2tog, knit to end of instep, ssk, knit to end of rnd. 2 sts decreased.
Rnd 2: Knit.

Note: For adjustable size, work these 2 rnds L times.

56 (60, 64, 68, 76, S) sts rem.

The Rest of the Foot

Once the gusset decreases are finished, remove all markers that aren't for the beginning of the round and continue:

Work in stockinette stitch until the foot of the sock is as long as you want, less the length needed for the toe, as follows:

If you are working the Short Sideways Toe, start toe shaping when your sock is 1½ (1½, 1¾, 1¾, 2, U)"/3.5 (4, 4, 4.5, 5, U) cm or 16 (17, 18, 19, 22, 0.275 × S) rnds shorter than the desired length of the sock.

If you are working the Medium Sideways Toe, start toe shaping when your sock is 1¾ (1¾, 2, 2, 2¼, U)"/4 (4.5, 5, 5, 5.5, U) cm or 18 (19, 21, 22, 24, 0.325 × S) rnds shorter than the desired length of the sock.

If you are working the Long Sideways Toe, start toe shaping when your sock is 2¼ (2½, 2¾, 2¾, 3, U)"/5.5 (6, 6.5, 7, 7.5, U) cm or 25 (26, 29, 30, 33, 0.45 × S) rnds shorter than the desired length of the sock.

Toe

Break color A. Join color B.

Set-up Rnd: K28 (30, 32, 34, 38, X) sts, pm, knit to end of rnd.

SHORT SIDEWAYS TOE

Rnd 1: K3 (3, 4, 4, 4, E), ssk, knit to 5 (5, 6, 6, 6, M) sts before marker, k2tog, k6 (6, 8, 8, 8, N), ssk, knit to 5 (5, 6, 6, 6, M) sts before marker, k2tog, knit to end of rnd. 4 sts decreased.

Rnd 2: Knit.

Rep Rnds 1 and 2 until you have 32 (36, 36, 40, 44, ~P) sts on the needles.

Then, rep only Rnd 1 until you have 16 (16, 20, 20, 20, ~D × 2) sts on the needles. K4 (4, 5, 5, 5, D/2); graft rem sts closed.

MEDIUM SIDEWAYS TOE

Rnd 1: K2 (2, 2, 2, 3, E), ssk, knit to 4 (4, 4, 4, 5, M) sts before marker, k2tog, k4 (4, 4, 4, 6, N), ssk, knit to 4 (4, 4, 4, 5, M) sts before marker, k2tog, knit to end of rnd. 4 sts decreased.

Rnd 2: Knit.

Rep Rnds 1 and 2 until you have 28 (32, 32, 36, 40, ~X) sts on the needles.

Then, rep only Rnd 1 until you have 12 (12, 12, 12, 16, ~D × 2) sts on the needles. K3 (3, 3, 3, 4, D/2); graft rem sts closed.

LONG SIDEWAYS TOE

Rnd 1: K2 (2, 2, 2, 3, E), ssk, knit to 4 (4, 4, 4, 5, M) sts before marker, k2tog, k4 (4, 4, 4, 6, N), ssk, knit to 4 (4, 4, 4, 5, M) sts before marker, k2tog, knit to end of rnd. 4 sts decreased.

Rnds 2 and 3: Knit.

Rep Rnds 1–3 until you have 28 (32, 32, 36, 40, ~X) sts on the needles.

Then, rep only Rnd 1 until you have 12 (12, 12, 12, 16, ~D × 2) sts on the needles. K3 (3, 3, 3, 4, D/2); graft rem sts closed.

Finishing

Weave in all ends and block gently.

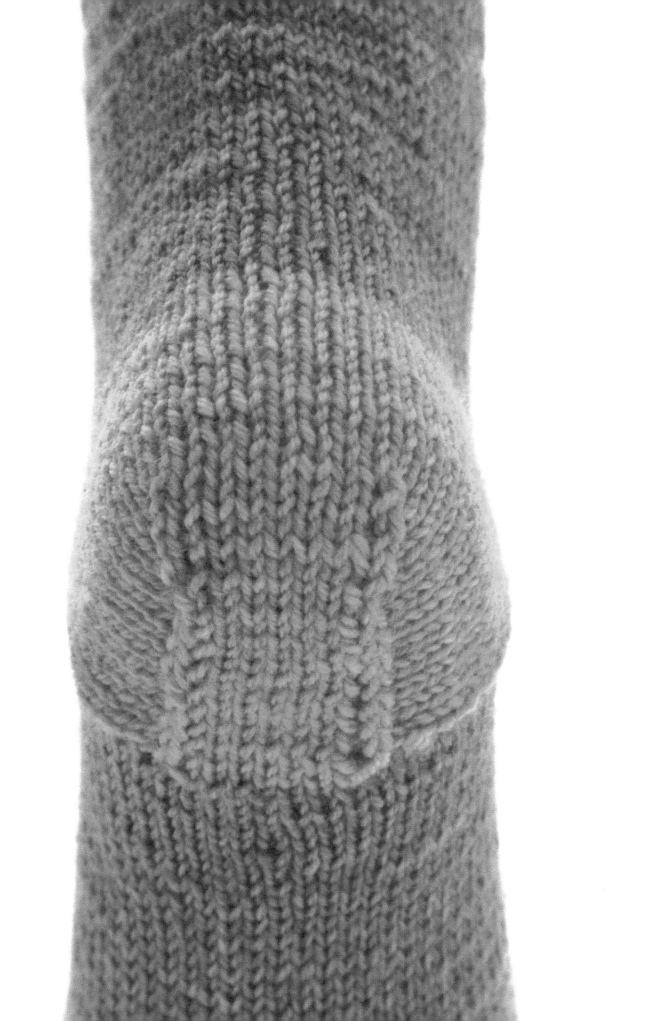

Dyad, Toe Up

SIZES

Women's XS (Women's S, Women's M/Men's S, Women's L/Men's M, Men's L, Adjustable Size)

FINISHED MEASUREMENTS

Foot circumference: 7 (7½, 8, 8½, 9½, U)"/18 (19, 20.5, 21.5, 24, U)cm

Finished leg length: adjustable to fit
Finished foot length: adjustable to fit

MATERIALS

Simply Socks Yarn Company Simply Sock Yarn (80% superwash wool, 20% nylon; 175 yds/160m per 50g skein)

With Gusset:
- [Color A] #646 Blue Skies; 2 skeins
- [Color B] #535 Wheatgrass; 1 skein

Without Gusset:
- [Color A] #535 Wheatgrass; 2 skeins
- [Color B] #646 Blue Skies; 1 skein

US #1 (2.25 mm) needles or size needed to achieve gauge

4 stitch markers
Yarn needle

I like to have a smaller, sharper needle at hand for working my lifted increases. It greatly reduces the stress on the yarn and my hands.

GAUGE

32 sts and 44 rnds = 4"/10 cm in stockinette stitch

PATTERN

Cast On and Toe

This begins like a wedge toe and is, essentially, a very wide wedge toe turned on its side. Choose the shape of toe you want to use. If you don't have a favorite, see page 13 for tips. All toes begin with Color B.

SHORT SIDEWAYS TOE

CO 16 (16, 20, 20, 20, D × 2) sts, using Judy's Magic Cast On. Knit 1 rnd.

Set-up Rnd 1: [Kfb, k6 (6, 8, 8, 8, N), kfb] twice. 20 (20, 24, 24, 24, CO + 4) sts on the needles.
Set-up Rnd 2: [K1, pm, k8 (8, 12, 12, 12, D), pm, k1] twice.

Rnd 1: [Knit to 1st marker, m1R, sm, knit to next marker, sm, m1L] twice, knit to end. 4 sts increased.
Rnd 2: Knit.

Rep only Rnd 1 until you have 32 (36, 36, 40, 44, ~P) sts on the needles.
Rep Rnds 1 and 2 until you have 56 (60, 64, 68, 76, S) sts on the needles.

WORKING OUT CUSTOM SIZING FOR DYAD, TOE UP

See page 49 for help with using this table. S must be divisible by 4.

Variable	How to calculate that variable	Write your result below
X	S/2	
B	X / 4 If X is odd, this needs to be odd. If X is even, this needs to be even.	
E	S + B − (X/2)	
C	X/2 + X/8 This needs to be a whole, even number.	
D	For Short Toes: D = (S × 0.3) / 2 = the number of stitches you will begin with on the top and bottom of your toe. This needs to be a whole, even number. For Medium and Long Toes: D = (S × 0.2) / 2 = the number of stitches you will begin with on the top and bottom of your toe. This needs to be a whole, even number.	
N	D − 2	
P	S × 0.6	

MEDIUM SIDEWAYS TOE

CO 12 (12, 12, 12, 16, D × 2) sts, using Judy's Magic Cast On. Knit 1 rnd.

Set-up Rnd 1: [Kfb, k4 (4, 4, 4, 6, N), kfb] twice. 16 (16, 16, 16, 20, CO + 4) sts on the needles.
Set-up Rnd 2: [K1, pm, k6 (6, 6, 6, 8, D), pm, k1] twice.

Rnd 1: [Knit to 1st marker, m1R, sm, knit to next marker, sm, m1L] twice, knit to end. 4 sts increased.
Rnd 2: Knit.

Rep only Rnd 1 until you have 28 (32, 32, 36, 40, ~X) sts on the needles.
Rep Rnds 1 and 2 until you have 56 (60, 64, 68, 76, S) sts on the needles.

LONG SIDEWAYS TOE

CO 12 (12, 12, 12, 16, D × 2) sts, using Judy's Magic Cast On. Knit 1 rnd.

Set-up Rnd 1: [Kfb, k4 (4, 4, 4, 6, N), kfb] twice. 16 (16, 16, 16, 20, CO + 4) sts on the needles.
Set-up Rnd 2: [K1, pm, k6 (6, 6, 6, 8, D), pm, k1] twice.

Rnd 1: [Knit to 1st marker, m1R, sm, knit to next marker, sm, m1L] twice, knit to end. 4 sts increased.
Rnds 2 and 3: Knit.

Rep only Rnd 1 until you have 28 (32, 32, 36, 40, ~X) sts on the needles.
Rep Rnds 1–3 until you have 56 (60, 64, 68, 76, S) sts on the needles.

Remove all stitch markers. Place one for the beginning of the round, if you like. It should be at the outer edge of the toe. Break color B. Join color A.

The Rest of the Foot

Work in stockinette stitch until the foot of the sock is as long as you want, less the length needed for the heel (and gusset, if you are working one).

If you are working the heel with a gusset (Option 1), the number of rounds required for the gusset shaping and heel turn is the same as half your foot stitches. So you should begin your

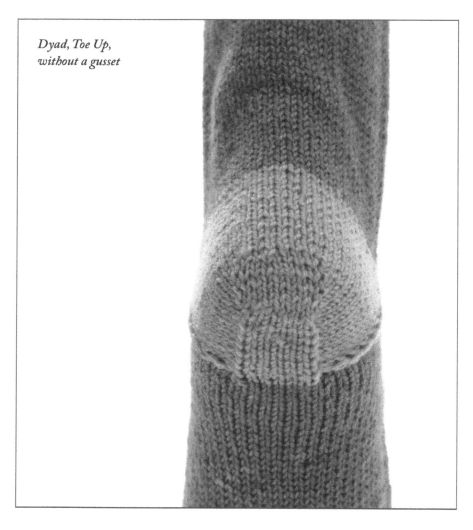

Dyad, Toe Up, without a gusset

gusset shaping when your sock foot is 2½ (2¾, 3, 3, 3½, X/11)"/6.5 (7, 7.5, 8, 8.5, X/4.4) cm or 28 (30, 32, 34, 38, X) rnds shorter than your desired total foot length.

If you are working the heel without a gusset (Option 2), your gusset shaping is worked as you are turning the heel. It hugs the foot very well, but may be too snug for some people. If you are worried that the area around the instep join will be too tight for the wearer, I strongly suggest test-knitting the heel shaping with about an inch of foot/leg before and after. Place the test heel on a piece of waste yarn or very flexible circular needle and try it on.

Option 2 takes 1¾ (1¾, 2, 2¼, 2½, 3X/44)"/4 (4.5, 5, 5.5, 6, 3X/17.6) cm or 18 (20, 22, 24, 26, 3X/4) rnds to work, so begin this option when your sock is that much shorter than desired.

I'll be frank. Option 2 can get rather strange when X/4 isn't automatically a whole number. Take lots of notes to avoid driving yourself absolutely bonkers.

Option 1: Band Heel, With Gusset

This version is shown in the photographs of the blue sock with the green heel.

GUSSET SHAPING

Pm halfway around your sock.

Rnd 1: Knit to marker, sm, m1L, knit to end of rnd, m1R. 2 sts increased.

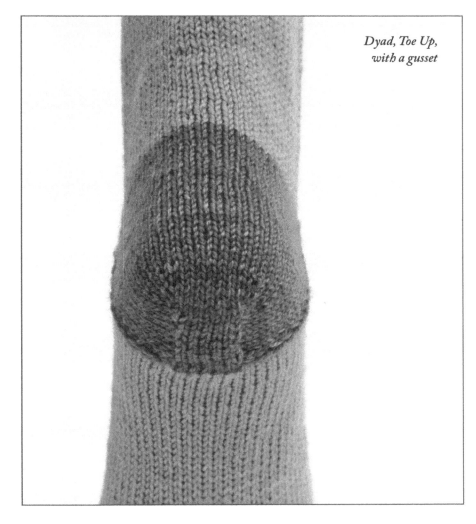

Dyad, Toe Up, with a gusset

Rnd 2: Knit.
Rep these 2 rnds until you have 64 (68, 72, 76, 86, S + B) sts. Break color A. Join color B.

HEEL TURN

This begins with a very small heel strap, which will lie under the wearer's heel. The strap is 8 (8, 8, 8, 10, B) sts wide.

Set-up Row: K50 (53, 56, 59, 67, E) sts. Turn. This takes you to the far side of the heel strap sts. From here, you'll be working back and forth over the 8 (8, 8, 10, B) heel strap sts.

Row 1 (WS): Sl1, p7 (7, 7, 7, 9, B–1). Turn.
Row 2 (RS): Sl1, k7 (7, 7, 7, 9, B–1). Turn.
Rep these 2 rows 7 (7, 7, 7, 9, B–1) times more. Work 1 more WS row. Break yarn.

With RS facing, join yarn to the lower right-hand side of the heel strap you just made and pick up and knit 8 (8, 8, 8, 10, B) sts, kfb, k6 (6, 6, 6, 8, B–2) sts, kfb, pick up and knit 8 (8, 8, 8, 10, B) sts. 26 (26, 26, 26, 32, 3B + 2) sts on the heel.

If this number is already equal to X, go to Close Heel Flap. Otherwise, continue as follows:

Slip 1 st back onto left needle, and work an ssk on this stitch and the one after it. Turn.

Set-up Row (WS): Sl1, pm, p8 (8, 8, 8, 10, B) sts, pm, p8 (8, 8, 8, 10, B) sts, pm, p8 (8, 8, 8, 10, B), pm, p2tog. Turn.

Row 1 (RS): Sl1, sm, knit to next marker, m1L, sm, knit to next marker, sm, m1R, knit to next marker, ssk. Turn.

Row 2 (WS): Sl 1, purl to fourth marker, p2tog. Turn.
Rep these 2 rows 0 (1, 2, 3, 2, U) times more. 26 (28, 30, 32, 36, X–2) sts between the first and fourth markers. Remove all markers.

CLOSE HEEL FLAP

Row 1 (RS): Sl1, k26 (28, 30, 32, 36, X–2) sts, ssk. Turn.
Row 2 (WS): Sl1, p26 (28, 30, 32, 36, X–2) sts, p2tog. Turn.
Rep these 2 rows until you have 56 (60, 64, 68, 76, S) sts, total. Break color B. Join color A.

Option 2: Band Heel, Without Gusset

This version is shown in the photographs of the green sock with the blue heel.

The heel is worked in three parts. Break color A. Join color B.

PART 1—HEEL STRAP

Set-up Row (RS): K18 (20, 20, 22, 24, C) sts. Turn.

Row 1 (WS): Sl1, p7 (7, 7, 7, 9, B–1). Turn.
Row 2 (RS): Sl1, k7 (7, 7, 7, 9, B–1). Turn.
Rep these 2 rows 7 (7, 7, 7, 9, B–1) times more. Break yarn.

PART 2

With RS facing, join yarn to the lower right-hand side of the heel strap you just made and pick up and knit 8 (8, 8, 8, 10, B) sts, kfb, k6 (6, 6, 6, 8, B–2) sts, kfb, pick up and knit 8 (8, 8, 8, 10, B) sts. 26 (26, 26, 26, 32, 3B + 2) sts on the heel.

If this number is already equal to X, go to Part 3. Otherwise, continue as follows:

Slip 1 st back onto left needle, and work an ssk on this stitch and the one after it. Turn.

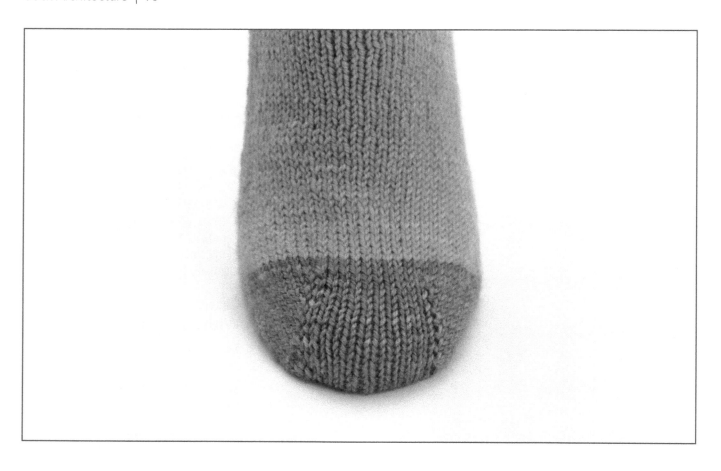

Set-up Row (WS): Sl1, pm, p8 (8, 8, 8, 10, B) sts, pm, p8 (8, 8, 8, 10, B) sts, pm, p8 (8, 8, 8, 10, B), pm, p2tog. Turn.

Row 1 (RS): Sl1, sm, knit to next marker, m1L, sm, knit to next marker, sm, m1R, knit to next marker, ssk. Turn.

Row 2 (WS): Sl1, purl to fourth marker, p2tog. Turn.

Rep these 2 rows 0 (1, 2, 3, 2, U) times more. 26 (28, 30, 32, 36, X–2) sts between the first and fourth markers. Remove all markers.

PART **3**

Row 1 (RS): Sl1, k26 (28, 30, 32, 36, X–2) sts, ssk. Turn.

Row 2 (WS): Sl1, p26 (28, 30, 32, 36, X–2) sts, p2tog. Turn.

Rep these two rows until you have 56 (60, 64, 68, 76, S) sts, total. Break color B. Join color A.

Leg and Bind Off

Work in stockinette stitch until leg is 2"/5 cm less than desired length.

Work [k2, p2] ribbing for 2"/5 cm.

BO. I like Jeny's Surprisingly Stretchy Bind Off, but any bind off that is stretchy enough for the sock to get over the foot will work. Please see page 47 for more information about bind offs for toe-up socks.

Finishing

Weave in all ends and block gently.

*Dyad, Toe Up,
with a gusset*

Procrastinatrix, Top Down

SIZES

Women's XS (Women's S, Women's M/Men's S, Women's L/Men's M, Men's L, Adjustable Size); shown in size Women's M

FINISHED MEASUREMENTS

Foot circumference: 7 (7½, 8, 8½, 9½, U)"/18 (19, 20.5, 21.5, 24, U) cm

Finished leg length: adjustable to fit
Finished foot length: adjustable to fit

MATERIALS

Simply Socks Yarn Company Simply Sock Yarn (80% superwash wool, 20% nylon; 175 yds/160m per 50g skein); color: #646 Blue Skies; 2 (2, 2, 2, 3, U) skeins

US#1 (2.25 mm) needles or size needed to achieve gauge

2 stitch markers
Waste yarn or a small spare needle for the extra needle technique
Yarn needle

GAUGE

32 sts and 44 rnds = 4"/10 cm in stockinette stitch

PATTERN NOTES

These instructions cover how to create this heel using waste yarn to hold stitches. To use the Extra Needle Technique, see page 29.

For more information and step-by-step photos of the Gusseted Afterthought Heel, see page 30.

PATTERN

To work out your own custom sizing to use in the instructions that follow, see page 100.

IN THIS SOCK, THE HEEL IS KNIT LAST, SO IT hints at a slight proclivity to procrastination. Hence, Procrastinatrix. Spellcheck may not like the name, but I sure do.

Everything about this sock is entirely run-of-the-mill and familiar, except for the order in which it is made. Amaze your friends and companions by turning what looks like a very strange sock indeed into one with a French heel.

If you love top-down French heels, but hate picking up stitches along the side of the heel flap, this is the heel for you. Decreases, not picked-up stitches, connect the heel flap to the gusset.

I used a slipped-stitch heel flap, for strength.

Cast On and Leg

CO 56 (60, 64, 68, 76, S) sts. Distribute sts among needles as you prefer, and join without twisting to work in the round.

Work [k1, p1] ribbing for 2"/5 cm.

Work in stockinette stitch until the leg is 2½ (2¾, 3, 3, 3½, X/11)"/6.5 (7, 7.5, 8, 8.5, X/4.4) cm shorter than your desired length to bottom of heel.

Gusset Cast On

Using waste yarn and an open provisional cast on, add 8 (9, 9, 10, 11, G/2) sts. Still using waste yarn, knit across 28 (30, 32, 34, 38, X) sts, then CO 8 (9, 9, 10, 11, G/2) more sts using the same open provisional cast on. Return to your working yarn and work across the stitches you cast on, the stitches knit with waste yarn, and the second group of cast-on stitches. Add a marker for the beginning of your instep stitches, then work the rest of the round. Your sock will have two little "ears" sticking out on either side. If you don't already

have a stitch marker for the beginning of the round, add one now. 72 (78, 82, 88, 98, B) sts.

Gusset Decreases

Rnd 1: Ssk, knit to 2 sts before the instep marker, k2tog, knit to end of rnd. 2 sts decreased.
Rnd 2: Knit.

Rep these 2 rnds until the sock has the same number of sts as it had on the leg, 56 (60, 64, 68, 76, S) sts.

The Rest of the Foot

Leave the stitch markers in place, and continue:

Work in stockinette stitch until the foot of the sock is as long as you want, less the total length needed for the toe and the heel turn, as follows:

If you are working the Short Wedge Toe, start toe shaping when your sock is 2½ (2¾, 3, 3, 3½, U)"/6.5 (6.5, 7.5, 7.5, 8.5, U) cm or 28 (29, 32, 33, 38, L) rnds shorter than the desired length of the sock.

WORKING OUT CUSTOM SIZING FOR PROCRASTINATRIX, TOP DOWN

See page 49 for help with using this table. S must be divisible by 4.

Variable	How to calculate that variable	Write your result below
X	S/2	
A	(X / 2) − 1	
R	(X − 4) / 2 Round down, if needed, so that R is an even number.	
G	X − R	
B	S + G	
I	S × 0.6 Round to nearest multiple of 4.	
J	S × 0.2 Round to nearest multiple of 4.	
K	S × 0.3 Round to nearest multiple of 4.	
L	The length of the toe you want (see below), in rounds, plus R, in rows	

The length of your sock toe will depend on which shape of toe you want:

- A short wedge toe will be about 0.275 × S rounds long.

- A medium wedge toe will be about 0.325 × S rounds long.

- A long wedge toe will be about .045 × S rounds long.

Take the length of the toe you want, in rounds, then divide that by your round gauge to get the approximate final length of your toe shaping.

If you are working the Medium Wedge Toe, start toe shaping when your sock is 2¾ (2¾, 3¼, 3¼, 3¾, U)"/7 (7, 8, 8, 9, U) cm or 30 (31, 35, 36, 40, L) rnds shorter than the desired length of the sock.

If you are working the Long Wedge Toe, start toe shaping when your sock is 3¼ (3½, 4, 4, 4½, U)"/ 8.5 (8.5, 10, 10, 11, U) cm or 37 (38, 43, 44, 49, L) rnds shorter than the desired length of the sock.

Toe

SHORT WEDGE TOE

Rnd 1: [Ssk, knit to 2 sts before marker, k2tog] twice. 4 sts decreased.
Rnd 2: Knit.

Rep Rnds 1 and 2 until you have 32 (36, 36, 40, 44, I) sts on the needles. Then, rep only Rnd 1 until you have 16 (16, 20, 20, 20, K) sts on the needles. Graft rem sts closed.

MEDIUM WEDGE TOE

Rnd 1: [Ssk, knit to 2 sts before marker, k2tog] twice. 4 sts decreased.
Rnd 2: Knit.

Rep Rnds 1 and 2 until you have 28 (32, 32, 36, 40, ~X) sts on the needles. Then, rep only Rnd 1 until you have 12 (12, 12, 12, 16, J) sts on the needles. Graft rem sts closed.

LONG WEDGE TOE

Rnd 1: [Ssk, knit to 2 sts before marker, k2tog] twice. 4 sts decreased.
Rnds 2 and 3: Knit.

Rep Rnds 1–3 until you have 28 (32, 32, 36, 40, ~X) sts on the needles. Then, rep only Rnd 1 until you have 12 (12, 12, 12, 16, J) sts on the needles. Graft rem sts closed.

Heel

Remove the waste yarn. Position the sock so that the top ribbing is pointed toward you and the toe is away from you. Slide your 28 (30, 32, 34, 38, X) heel flap sts, which will be live sts closest to you, onto working needles. Place the 44 (48, 50, 54, 60, X + G) other sts, which will be on the foot side of the sock, on spare needles.

Heel Flap

For the heel flap, you will work back and forth, using decreases on either side of the flap to close it to the gusset stitches. You will have to juggle stitches from one needle to another before working each decrease. Join yarn on the right edge of the heel flap stitches.

Row 1 (RS): [Sl1, k1] 13 (14, 15, 16, 18, A) times, sl1, ssk.
Row 2 (WS): Sl1, p26 (28, 30, 32, 36, X–2), p2tog.
Rep these 2 rows 13 (14, 15, 16, 18, A) more times. You should have 28 (30, 32, 34, 38, X) sts on your working needles and 16 (18, 18, 20, 22, G) sts still on spare needles.

Heel Turn

Row 1 (RS): Sl1, k14 (15, 16, 17, 19, X/2), ssk, k1. Turn.
Row 2 (WS): Sl1, p5, p2tog, p1. Turn.

Row 3: Sl1, k6, ssk, k1. Turn.
Row 4: Sl1, p7, p2tog, p1. Turn.

Continue in patt as set, working 1 more stitch before the decrease in each row, until you have worked all of the heel sts. 16 (18, 18, 20, 22, G) sts on the working needles. Graft these sts to the ones still on hold. Use a darning needle to close any gaps at the top of the heel flap.

Finishing

Weave in all ends and block gently.

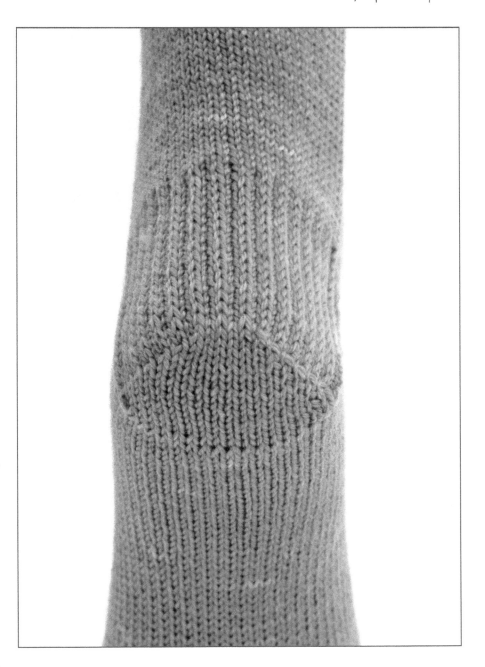

Procrastinatrix, Toe Up

SIZES

Women's XS (Women's S, Women's M/
Men's S, Women's L/Men's M, Men's
L, Adjustable Size); shown in size
Women's M

FINISHED MEASUREMENTS

Foot circumference: 7 (7½, 8, 8½, 9½,
U)"/18 (19, 20.5, 21.5, 24, U) cm

Finished leg length: adjustable to fit
Finished foot length: adjustable to fit

MATERIALS

Simply Socks Yarn Company Simply
Sock Yarn (80% superwash wool, 20%
nylon; 175 yds/160m per 50g skein)
- [Color A] #646 Blue Skies;
  2 skeins
- [Color B] #535 Wheatgrass;
  1 skein

US#1 (2.25 mm) needles or size
needed to achieve gauge

2 stitch markers
Waste yarn or a small spare needle for
the extra needle technique
Yarn needle

GAUGE

32 sts and 44 rnds = 4"/10 cm in stockinette stitch

PATTERN NOTES

These instructions cover how to create
this heel using waste yarn to hold
stitches. To use the Extra Needle
Technique, see page 29.

For more information and step-by-step
photos of the Gusseted Afterthought
Heel, see page 30.

PATTERN

To work out your own custom sizing to
use in the instructions that follow, see
page 104.

A S YOU MIGHT GUESS, THIS IS VERY
similar to the Procrastinatrix Socks that are
knit from the top down. I added a little color
change into these: heels, toes and ribbing are
in a contrasting color.

I've never managed to get grafted stitches at the top of
a heel flap to look quite as nice as I would like, so even
though this sock is knit from the toe up, the heel is knit
from the top down. It's a bit of a twist and is only really
possible with this style of construction.

If you need any more convincing to try a toe-up sock, with
this version you can avoid casting on gusset stitches. In
many ways, it is the best of both worlds.

Cast On and Toe

Choose the shape of toe you want to
use. If you don't have a favorite, see
page 38 for tips.

SHORT WEDGE TOE

With color B, CO 16 (20, 20, 20, 20,
K) sts, using Judy's Magic Cast On.
Knit 1 rnd, placing a marker for beginning of rnd and another one halfway
around your toe.

Rnd 1: K1, m1L, knit to 1 st before
marker, m1R, k1, sm, k1, m1L, knit to
1 st before end of rnd, m1R, k1. 4 sts
increased.
Rep this rnd until you have 32 (36, 36,
40, 44, I) sts on the needles.

Rnd 1: K1, m1L, knit to 1 st before
marker, m1R, k1, sm, k1, m1L, knit to
1 st before end of rnd, m1R, k1. 4 sts
increased.
Rnd 2: Knit.
Rep these 2 rnds until you have 56 (60,
64, 68, 76, S) sts on the needles.

MEDIUM WEDGE TOE

With color B, CO 12 (12, 12, 16, 16,
J) sts, using Judy's Magic Cast On. Pm
for beginning of rnd and another one
halfway around your toe.

Rnd 1: K1, m1L, knit to 1 st before
marker, m1R, k1, sm, k1, m1L, knit to
1 st before end of rnd, m1R, k1. 4 sts
increased.
Rep this rnd until you have 28 (32, 32,
36, 40, ~X) sts on the needles.

Rnd 1: K1, m1L, knit to 1 st before
marker, m1R, k1, sm, k1, m1L, knit to
1 st before end of rnd, m1R, k1. 4 sts
increased.
Rnd 2: Knit.
Rep these 2 rnds until you have 56 (60,
64, 68, 76, S) sts on the needles.

LONG WEDGE TOE

With color B, CO 12 (12, 12, 16, 16,
J) sts, using Judy's Magic Cast On. Pm
for beginning of rnd and another one
halfway around your toe.

Rnd 1: K1, m1L, knit to 1 st before
marker, m1R, k1, sm, k1, m1L, knit to
1 st before end of rnd, m1R, k1. 4 sts
increased.

Rep this rnd until you have 28 (32, 32, 36, 40, ~X) sts on the needles.

Rnd 1: K1, m1L, knit to 1 st before marker, m1R, k1, sm, k1, m1L, knit to 1 st before end of rnd, m1R, k1. 4 sts increased.
Rnds 2–3: Knit.
Rep these 3 rnds until you have 56 (60, 64, 68, 76, S) sts on the needles.

The Rest of the Foot

Once the toe increases are finished, leave stitch markers in place, and continue. Break color B, join color A. Work in stockinette stitch until the foot of the sock is as long as you want, less the length needed for the gusset and heel shaping: 2½ (2¾, 3, 3, 3½, X/11)"/6.5 (7, 7.5, 8, 8.5, X/4.4) cm or 28 (30, 32, 34, 38, X) rows long.

Gusset

Rnd 1: Knit to marker, sm, m1L, knit to end of rnd, m1R. 2 sts increased.

Rnd 2: Knit.
Rep these 2 rnds until you have added 16 (18, 18, 20, 22, G) sts. 72 (78, 82, 88, 98, B) sts total.

Slip 8 (9, 9, 10, 11, G/2) sts onto waste yarn. With waste yarn, knit across 28 (32, 32, 36, 40, X) sts. Slip 8 (9, 9, 10, 11, G/2) sts onto waste yarn. Return to your working yarn, knit across the stitches you knit with waste yarn. You will have two little "ears" of on-hold stitches sticking out from the edges of your sock.

Leg

Work in stockinette stitch until the leg is 4"/10 cm less than desired length, measured from the waste yarn. Break color A. Join color B.

Work [k1, p1] ribbing for 2"/5 cm.

BO. I like Jeny's Surprisingly Stretchy Bind Off, but any bind off that is stretchy enough for the sock to get

over the foot will work. Please see page 47 for more information about bind offs for toe-up socks.

Heel

Remove the waste yarn. Position the sock so that the top ribbing is pointed toward you and the toe is away from you. Slide your 28 (30, 32, 34, 38, X) heel flap stitches, which will be live stitches closest to you, onto working needles. Place the 44 (48, 50, 54, 60, X + G) other sts, which will be on the foot side of the sock, on spare needles.

Heel Flap

For the heel flap, you will work back and forth, using decreases on either side of the flap to close it to the gusset stitches. You will have to juggle stitches from one needle to another before working each decrease. Join color B on the right edge of the heel flap stitches.

Row 1 (RS): [Sl1, k1] 13 (14, 15, 16, 18, A) times, sl1, ssk.
Row 2 (WS): Sl1, p26 (28, 30, 32, 36, X–2), p2tog.
Rep these 2 rows 13 (14, 15, 16, 18, A) more times. You should have 28 (30, 32, 34, 38, X) sts on your working needles and 16 (18, 18, 20, 22, G) sts still on spare needles.

Heel Turn

Row 1 (RS): Sl1, k14 (15, 16, 17, 19, X/2), ssk, k1. Turn.
Row 2 (WS): Sl1, p5, p2tog, p1. Turn.
Row 3: Sl1, k6, ssk, k1. Turn.
Row 4: Sl1, p7, p2tog, p1. Turn.

Continue in patt as set, working 1 more stitch before the decrease in each row, until you have worked all of the heel sts. 16 (18, 18, 20, 22, G) sts on the working needles. Graft these sts to the ones still on hold. Use a darning needle to close any gaps at the top of the heel flap.

Finishing

Weave in all ends and block gently.

WORKING OUT CUSTOM SIZING FOR PROCRASTINATRIX, TOE UP

See page 49 for help with using this table. S must be divisible by 4.

Variable	How to calculate that variable	Write your result below
X	S/2	
A	(X / 2) − 1	
R	(X − 4) / 2 Round down, if needed, so that R is an even number.	
G	X − R	
B	S + G	
I	S × 0.6 Round to nearest multiple of 4.	
J	S × 0.2 Round to nearest multiple of 4.	
K	S × 0.3 Round to nearest multiple of 4.	

Sidle, Top Down

SIZES

Women's XS (Women's S, Women's M/ Men's S, Women's L/Men's M, Men's L, Adjustable Size); shown in size Women's M

FINISHED MEASUREMENTS

Foot circumference: 7 (7½, 8, 8½, 9½, U)"/18 (19, 20.5, 21.5, 24, U) cm

Finished leg length: adjustable to fit
Finished foot length: adjustable to fit

MATERIALS

Simply Socks Yarn Company Simply Sock Yarn (80% superwash wool, 20% nylon; 175 yds/160m per 50g skein); color: #646 Blue Skies; 2 (2, 2, 2, 3, U) skeins

US#1 (2.25 mm) needles or size needed to achieve gauge

3 stitch markers
Scrap yarn (optional)
Yarn needle

GAUGE

32 sts and 44 rnds = 4"/10 cm in stockinette stitch

PATTERN

To work out your own custom sizing to use in the instructions that follow, see page 108.

Cast On and Leg

CO 56 (60, 64, 68, 76, S) sts. Distribute sts among needles as you prefer, and join without twisting to work in the round.

Work [k1, p1] ribbing for 2"/5 cm.

Work in stockinette stitch until the leg is as long as you want, as measured from the bottom of the heel, less the calculated length of the heel/toe.

"To sidle" means to walk up to someone, usually in a furtive or sneaky manner. These socks aren't made in a sideways fashion, but the heel and toe are both 90 degrees from what you might expect, and they are pretty enough to surprise. The afterthought heel is worked in exactly the same way as the toe. There is no gusset for this sock.

Set Up the Heel

SCRAP YARN, EXTRA NEEDLE, OR SNIP?

If you wish, you can choose to work the stitches of the heel with a length of scrap yarn, for easy removal later. Or if you're feeling brave—or you don't know where you want the heel to be—just keep working, and you'll snip a strand later, to open up the sock.

To add scrap yarn, drop your working yarn. Using your scrap yarn (I like to use a different color to make it easier to see, but you could use a little bit of your working yarn from the other end of the ball), knit across 28 (30, 32, 34, 38, X) sts. Return to the start of the round by slipping the sts you just knit back onto the left-hand needle. Pick up your working yarn again, and continue working as before.

There is a third option. Instead of scrap yarn, you can leave behind an extra needle or two to hold your stitches. See the Extra Needle Technique section on page 29 for help with this.

The Rest of the Foot

Continue in stockinette stitch until the foot of the sock is as long as you want, less the total length needed for the toe and heel, as follows:

If you are working the Short Sideways Toe and Heel, start toe shaping when your sock is 3 (3, 3¼, 3½, 4, U)"/7.5 (8, 8, 8.5, 10, U) cm or 32 (34, 36, 38, 44,

---

0.55 × S) rnds shorter than the desired length of the foot, measured from the scrap yarn or tiny needle.

If you are working the Medium Sideways Toe and Heel, start toe shaping when your sock is 3¼ (3½, 3¾, 4, 4¼, U)"/8 (8.5, 9.5, 10, 11, U) cm or 36 (38, 42, 44, 48, 0.65 × S) rnds shorter than the desired length of the foot, measured from the scrap yarn or tiny needle.

If you are working the Long Sideways Toe and Heel, start toe shaping when your sock is 4½ (4¾, 5¼, 5½, 6, U)"/11.5 (12, 13, 13.5, 15, U) cm or 50 (52, 58, 60, 66, 0.9 × S) rnds shorter than the desired length of the foot, measured from the scrap yarn or tiny needle.

Toe/Heel

Set-up Rnd: K14 (15, 16, 17, 19, X/2). Pm to mark new beginning of rnd. K28 (30, 32, 34, 38, X) sts, pm for middle of rnd, knit to end of rnd.

SHORT SIDEWAYS TOE

Rnd 1: K3 (3, 4, 4, 4, E), ssk, knit to 5 (5, 6, 6, 6, M) sts before marker, k2tog, k6 (6, 8, 8, 8, N), ssk, knit to 5 (5, 6, 6, 6, M) sts before marker, k2tog, knit to end of rnd. 4 sts decreased.
Rnd 2: Knit.

Rep these 2 rnds until you have 32 (36, 36, 40, 44, ~P) sts on the needles.

Then, rep only Rnd 1 until you have 16 (16, 20, 20, 20, ~D×2) sts on the needles. K4 (4, 5, 5, 5, D/2), graft rem sts closed.

MEDIUM SIDEWAYS TOE

Rnd 1: K2 (2, 2, 2, 3, E), ssk, knit to 4 (4, 4, 4, 5, M) sts before marker, k2tog, k4 (4, 4, 4, 6, N), ssk, knit to 4 (4, 4, 4, 5, M) sts before marker, k2tog, knit to end of rnd. 4 sts decreased.
Rnd 2: Knit.

Rep these 2 rnds until you have 28 (32, 32, 36, 40, ~X) sts on the needles.

Then, rep only Rnd 1 until you have 12 (12, 12, 12, 16, ~D×2) sts on the needles. K3 (3, 3, 3, 4, D/2), graft rem sts closed.

LONG SIDEWAYS TOE

Rnd 1: K2 (2, 2, 2, 3, E), ssk, knit to 4 (4, 4, 4, 5, M) sts before marker, k2tog, k4 (4, 4, 4, 6, N), ssk, knit to 4 (4, 4, 4, 5, M) sts before marker, k2tog, knit to end of rnd. 4 sts decreased.
Rnds 2 and 3: Knit.

Rep these 3 rnds until you have 28 (32, 32, 36, 40, ~X) sts on the needles.

Then, rep only Rnd 1 until you have 12 (12, 12, 12, 16, ~D×2) sts on the needles. K3 (3, 3, 3, 4, D/2), graft rem sts closed.

Add Heel

Return to the heel area of your sock. If you used it, simply pick out the scrap yarn stitches and place your newly-live stitches on needles or slide live stitches from your extra needle onto working needles. For the brave who didn't use either, decide where you want the heel to go by taking the total length wanted for the foot and subtracting the actual length of your finished toe. Snip a stitch in the center of what would be the half-round at the start of your heel. Pick out stitches in both directions until you have the number of stitches needed for the heel, sliding the newly-free stitches onto working needles and go from there.

A problem some knitters have with afterthought heels is holes at the corners, where the yarn of the picked-up stitches leaps from one side of the sock to the other. One way to handle this is to pick up two or three stitches to cover the gap, then decrease them away as you work the heel.

Join yarn at the outer corner of your heel (either corner will do). Make your heel by following the same instructions you used for your toe.

Finishing

Weave in all ends and block gently.

WORKING OUT CUSTOM SIZING FOR SIDLE, TOP DOWN

See page 49 for help with using this table. S must be divisible by 2.

Variable	How to calculate that variable	Write your result below
D	For Short Toes/Heels: $D = (S \times 0.3) / 2$ For Medium and Long Toes/Heels: $D = (S \times 0.2) / 2$ In all cases, round result to the nearest whole, even number.	
E	$(D / 2) - 1$	
M	$(D / 2) + 1$	
N	$D - 2$	
P	$S \times 0.6$	
U	Use U when you need to figure out the length of your toe/heel shaing. Make sure you're working with an even number of rounds. For Short Toes/Heels: $U = (0.55 \times S) /$ your round gauge For Medium Toes/Heels: $U = (0.65 \times S) /$ your round gauge For Long Toes/Heels: $U = (0.9 \times S) /$ your round gauge	

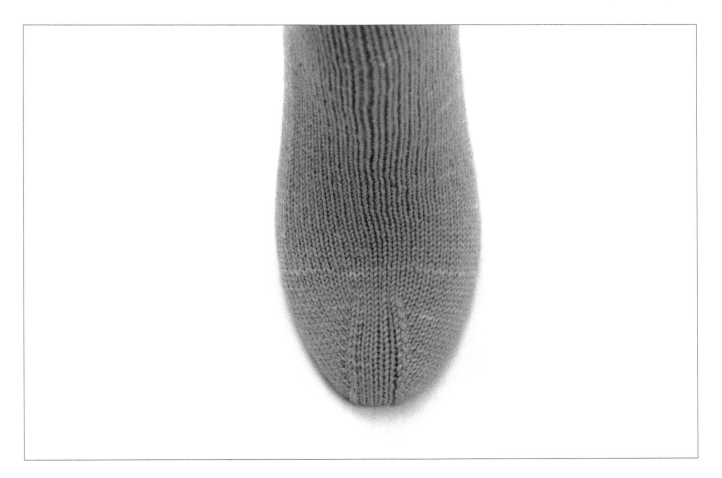

Sidle, Toe Up

SIZES

Women's XS (Women's S, Women's M/
Men's S, Women's L/Men's M, Men's
L, Adjustable Size)

FINISHED MEASUREMENTS

Foot circumference: 7 (7½, 8, 8½, 9½,
U)"/18 (19, 20.5, 21.5, 24, U) cm

Finished leg length: adjustable to fit
Finished foot length: adjustable to fit

MATERIALS

Simply Socks Yarn Company Simply
Sock Yarn (80% superwash wool, 20%
nylon; 175 yds/160m per 50g skein);
color: #350 Bittersweet; 2 (2, 2, 2, 3, U)
skeins

US#1 (2.25 mm) needles or size
needed to achieve gauge

5 stitch markers
Yarn needle
Small amount of extra yarn in the same
weight as your working yarn or a spare,
tiny circular needle.

I like to have a smaller, sharper needle
at hand for working my lifted increases.
It greatly reduces the stress on the yarn
and my hands. For this sock, you can
use the same small, circular needle for
the lifted increases and the extra needle
trick.

GAUGE

32 sts and 44 rnds = 4"/10 cm in stockinette stitch

PATTERN

To work out your own custom sizing to
use in the instructions that follow, see
page 112.

Cast On and Toe

This begins like a wedge toe and is,
essentially, a very wide wedge toe
turned on its side. Choose the shape of
toe you want to use. If you don't have
a favorite, see page 13 for tips.short
sideways toe

CO 16 (16, 20, 20, 20, D × 2) sts, using
Judy's Magic Cast On. Knit 1 rnd.

Set-up Rnd 1: [Kfb, k6 (6, 8, 8, 8, N),
kfb] twice. 20 (20, 24, 24, 24, CO+4)
sts on the needles.
Set-up Rnd 2: [K1, pm, k8 (8, 10, 10,
10, D), pm, k1] twice.

Rnd 1: [Knit to 1st marker, m1R, sm,
knit to next marker, sm, m1L] twice,
knit to end. 4 sts increased.
Rnd 2: Knit.

Rep only Rnd 1 until you have 32 (36,
36, 40, 44, ~P) sts on the needles.
Rep Rnds 1 and 2 until you have 56
(60, 64, 68, 76, S) sts on the needles.

MEDIUM SIDEWAYS TOE

CO 12 (12, 12, 12, 16, D × 2) sts, using
Judy's Magic Cast On. Knit 1 rnd.

Set-up Rnd 1: [Kfb, k4 (4, 4, 4, 6, N),
kfb] twice. 16 (16, 16, 16, 20, CO+4)
sts on the needles.
Set-up Rnd 2: [K1, pm, k6 (6, 6, 6, 8,
D), pm, k1] twice.

Rnd 1: [Knit to 1st marker, m1R, sm,
knit to next marker, sm, m1L] twice,
knit to end. 4 sts increased.
Rnd 2: Knit.

Rep only Rnd 1 until you have 28 (32,
32, 36, 40, ~X) sts on the needles.
Rep Rnds 1 and 2 until you have 56
(60, 64, 68, 76, S) sts on the needles.

LONG SIDEWAYS TOE

CO 12 (12, 12, 12, 16, D×2) sts, using
Judy's Magic Cast On. Knit 1 rnd.

Set-up Rnd 1: [Kfb, k4 (4, 4, 4, 6, N),
kfb] twice. 16 (16, 16, 16, 20, CO+4)
sts on the needles.
Set-up Rnd 2: [K1, pm, k6 (6, 6, 6, 8,
D), pm, k1] twice.

Rnd 1: [Knit to 1st marker, m1R, sm,
knit to next marker, sm, m1L] twice,
knit to end. 4 sts increased.
Rnds 2 and 3: Knit.

Rep only Rnd 1 until you have 28 (32,
32, 36, 40, ~X) sts on the needles.
Rep Rnds 1-3 until you have 56 (60,
64, 68, 76, S) sts on the needles.

All toe types: Remove all stitch markers,
and pm for beginning of rnd, if desired.
It should be at the outer edge of the
toe.

The Rest of the Foot

Work in stockinette stitch until the
foot of the sock is as long as you want,
less the length needed for the heel.

You can avoid working any math at
all to find the position of the heel
by taking a few measurements. The
heel and toe are made with the same
number of rows, so they are the same
length. After you have made the toe,
measure its length very carefully.

As with the top-down version of
this sock, there is no gusset here, but the
large heel will help it fit a variety of feet very
well. It is possible to nearly completely avoid
math in this toe-up version.

The fit of the toe is very similar to a medium wedge toe,
and even begins in the same way.

Continue to knit the sock, with no shaping, and place the heel when the foot is the length you want it, minus the length of the heel (which is the same length as the toe.)

If you are brave, you can avoid even this much thought and trouble as you knit. Make your sock with abandon, working away and ignoring the heel. See the "Set Up the Heel" and "Add Heel" instructions in the Sidle Socks, Top Down pattern on page 106.

Leg and Bind Off

Work in stockinette stitch leg is as long as you like, less 2"/5 cm plus the length you will gain when you add the heel, as follows:

WORKING OUT CUSTOM SIZING FOR SIDLE, TOE UP

See page 49 for help with using this table. S must be divisible by 2.

Variable	How to calculate that variable	Write your result below
D	For Short Toes/Heels: D = (S × 0.3) / 2 For Medium and Long Toes/Heels: D = (S × 0.2) / 2 In all cases, round result to the nearest whole, even number. Round up or down until S − (D × 2) = a multiple of 4.	
N	D − 2	
P	S × 0.6	
U	Use U when you need to figure out the length of your toe/heel shaing. Make sure you're working with an even number of rounds. For Short Toes/Heels: U = (0.275 × S) / your round gauge For Medium Toes/Heels: U = (0.325 × S) / your round gauge For Long Toes/Heels: U = (0.45 × S) / your round gauge	

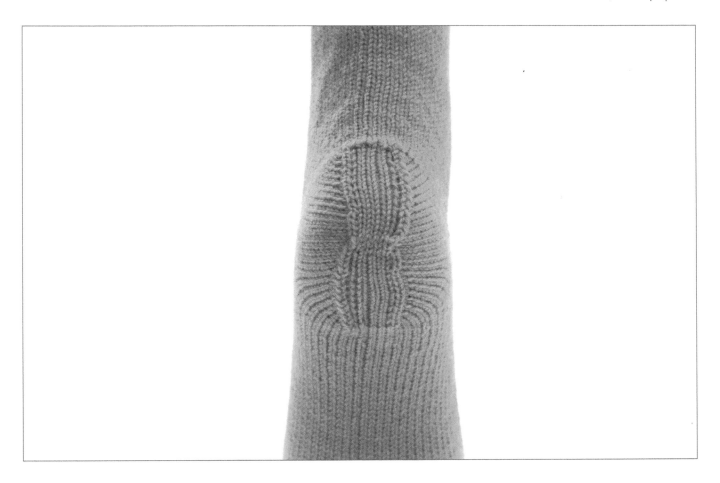

If working the Short Sideways Heel, it will add 1½ (1½, 1¾, 1¾, 2, U)"/3.5 (4, 4, 4.5, 5, U) cm or 16 (17, 18, 19, 22, 0.275 × S) rnds.

If working the Medium Sideways Heel, it will add 1¾ (1¾, 2, 2, 2¼, U)"/4 (4.5, 5, 5, 5.5, U) cm or 18 (19, 21, 22, 24, 0.325 × S) rnds.

If working the Long Sideways Heel, it will add 2¼ (2½, 2¾, 2¾, 3, U)"/5.5 (6, 6.5, 7, 7.5, U) cm or 25 (26, 29, 30, 33, 0.45 × S) rnds.

Work [k1, p1] ribbing for 2"/5 cm.

BO. I like Jeny's Surprisingly Stretchy Bind Off, but any bind off that is stretchy enough for the sock to get over the foot will work. Please see page 47 for more information about bind offs for toe-up socks.

Add Heel

Please see "Add Heel" instructions in the Sidle Socks, Top Down pattern on page 108, then follow the appropriate sideways toe instructions on page 107.

Finishing

Weave in all ends and block gently.

Arithmophobia, Top Down

Sizes

Women's XS (Women's S, Women's M/
Men's S, Women's L/Men's M, Men's
L, Adjustable Size); shown in size
Women's M.

Finished Measurements

Foot circumference: 7 (7½, 8, 8½, 9½,
U)"/ 18 (19, 20.5, 21.5, 24, U) cm

Finished leg length: adjustable to fit
Finished foot length: adjustable to fit

Materials

Simply Socks Yarn Company Simply
Sock Yarn (80% superwash wool, 20%
nylon; 175 yds/160m per 50g skein);
color: #646 Blue Skies; 2 (2, 2, 2, 3, U)
skeins

US#1 (2.25 mm) needles or size
needed to achieve gauge

1 stitch marker
Yarn needle

I like to have a smaller, sharper needle
at hand for working my lifted increases.
It greatly reduces the stress on the yarn
and my hands.

Gauge

32 sts and 44 rnds = 4"/10 cm in
stockinette stitch

Pattern

To work out your own custom sizing to
use in the instructions that follow, see
page 116.

Cast On and Leg

CO 56 (60, 64, 68, 76, S) sts. Distribute
sts among your needles as you prefer,
and join without twisting to work in
the round.

Work in [k1, p1] ribbing for 2"/5 cm.

Work in stockinette stitch until leg
measures 2"/5 cm less than desired to
bottom of heel.

"ARITHMOPHOBIA," ACCORDING TO
some people, is just a made-up word.
Others say it means "fear of math."
Either way, I think it sounds cool.

This pair of socks, if you follow the sized instructions, has
no math involved AT ALL. The heel and toe are identical, so
you can measure the length of the heel and start your toe
at the correct length with no problems.

The heel/toe is worked entirely in short-rows, with no fuss,
muss, stitch markers or wraps. Simple increases, followed
by even-more-simple decreases, prevent any gaps.

This makes a heel that fits a lot like a machine-made sock.
It's a good first-sock technique, because you can use the
same method for both the heel and the toe of your socks.
There are no gusset stitches. For a real in-depth look at
short-row heels and toes, get a copy of Priscilla Gibson-
Roberts' Simple Socks Plain and Fancy. It's a wonderful
book and really explores the design potential inherent in
this easy-to-knit style.

There are many ways to work a short-row heel/toe. My
favorite uses increases on the shorter short rows and
decreases on the longer short rows. (I know, it seems kind
of backwards, but stay with me.)

These instructions work for narrow, medium and wide
short-row heels and toes. The only change for each one is
when the shorter short rows become the longer short rows,
and how many stitches are involved at the turn.

Heel Turn

The heel will be worked flat across half
the stitches. Just ignore the other half
of the stitches (the instep stitches) and
let them sit on the needles unworked
until the heel is finished and it's time to
work the foot.

Shorter Short Row 1 (RS): Sl1, k27
(29, 31, 33, 37, X–1), m1L. Turn.
Shorter Short Row 2 (WS): Sl1, p26
(28, 30, 32, 36, X–2) m1P. Turn.

FOR A NARROW HEEL/TOE:

Continue in patt as set by the Shorter Short rows, working one less stitch on each row before making your increase, until you work a row where you purl 10 (10, 10, 12, 12, T) sts.

Then:
Turning Row 1 (RS): Sl1, k9 (9, 9, 11, 11, T–1), ssk, k1. Turn.
Turning Row 2 (WS): Sl1, p9 (9, 9, 11, 11, T–1), p2tog, p1. Turn.

Longer Short Row 1 (RS): Sl1, k10 (10, 10, 12, 12, T), ssk, k1. Turn.
Longer Short Row 2 (WS): Sl1, p11 (11, 11, 13, 13, T+1), p2tog, p1. Turn.

Proceed to "For All Styles."

FOR A MEDIUM HEEL/TOE:

Continue in patt as set by the Shorter Short rows, working 1 less stitch on each row before making your increase, until you work a row where you purl 14 (16, 16, 16, 20, T) sts.

Then:
Turning Row 1 (RS): Sl1, k13 (15, 15, 15, 19, T–1), ssk, k1. Turn.
Turning Row 2 (WS): Sl1, p13 (15, 15, 15, 19, T–1), p2tog, p1. Turn.

Longer Short Row 1 (RS): Sl1, k14 (16, 16, 16, 20, T), ssk, k1. Turn.
Longer Short Row 2 (WS): Sl1, p15, (17, 17, 17, 21, T+1), p2tog, p1. Turn.

Proceed to "For All Styles."

FOR A WIDE HEEL/TOE:

Continue in patt as set by the Shorter Short rows, working one less stitch on each row before making your increase, until you work a row where you purl 18 (20, 22, 22, 26, T) sts.

Then:
Turning Row 1 (RS): Sl1, k17 (19, 21, 21, 25, T–1), ssk, k1. Turn.
Turning Row 2 (WS): Sl1, p17 (19, 21, 21, 25, T–1), p2tog, p1. Turn.

Longer Short Row 1 (RS): Sl1, k18 (20, 22, 22, 26, T), ssk, k1. Turn.
Longer Short Row 2 (WS): Sl1, p19 (21, 23, 23, 27, T+1), p2tog, p1. Turn.

Proceed to "For All Styles."

If you are working one style of heel and a different style of toe, direct measurement of your heel depth needs a slight modification. Take the number of stitches purled on Turning Row 2 for your heel, and subtract the number of stitches purled on the 2nd turning row for your planned toe. That's how many more (or fewer) rows your toe will have before the first turning row than your heel did. When measuring the heel to see how long your toe will be, simply add a marker that many rows deeper into the foot of the sock than your actual heel shaping (or shy of the last heel shaping row), and measure.

FOR ALL STYLES

Rep the longer short rows, working one more stitch on each row before making your decrease, until you have worked all of your active heel sts, ending with a WS row. 28 (30, 32, 34, 38, X) sts. Turn, pm for beginning of rnd, and knit across the working sts. Continue knitting across the sts left on hold when you started working the heel.

The Rest of the Foot

Work in stockinette stitch until the foot is as long as you want, less the length needed for the toe. How long is your toe? Measure the length of the heel from the first shorter short row to the first turning row. That is the length of your toe.

Toe

Work exactly as for the heel. When finished, graft your live stitches to the 28 (30, 32, 34, 38, X) live stitches you put on hold while working the toe.

Finishing

Weave in all ends and block gently.

WORKING OUT CUSTOM SIZING FOR ARITHMOPHOBIA, TOP DOWN

See page 49 for help with using this table. S must be divisible by 2.

For a narrow heel/toe: Determine S/6 sts. Round up or down to the nearest whole number. Let's call this T. This heel/toe will take S/3 rows to work before the first turning row. If you want to know how deep that is in inches or centimeters, divide S/3 by your row/round gauge.

For a medium heel/toe: Determine S/4 sts. Round up or down to the nearest whole number. Let's call this T. This heel/toe will take S/4 rows to work before the first turning row. If you want to know how deep that is in inches or centimeters, divide S/4 by your row/round gauge.

For a wide heel/toe: Determine S/3 sts. Round up or down to the nearest whole number. Let's call this T. This heel/toe will take S/6 rows to work before the first turning row. If you want to know how deep that is in inches or centimeters, divide S/6 by your row/round gauge. At some gauges, this heel/toe will be extremely short. It might work great for a toe, but it may really be too shallow for a heel. You might want to choose a medium or narrow heel.

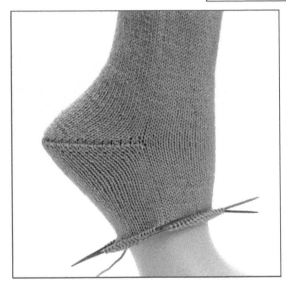

Arithmophobia, Toe Up

SIZES

Women's XS (Women's S, Women's M/Men's S, Women's L/Men's M, Men's L, Adjustable Size); shown in size Women's M

FINISHED MEASUREMENTS

Foot circumference: 7 (7½, 8, 8½, 9½, U)"/ 18 (19, 20.5, 21.5, 24, U) cm

Finished leg length: adjustable to fit
Finished foot length: adjustable to fit

MATERIALS

Simply Socks Yarn Company Simply Sock Yarn (80% superwash wool, 20% nylon; 175 yds/160m per 50g skein); color: #205 Cranberry; 2 (2, 2, 2, 3, U) skeins

US#1 (2.25 mm) needles or size needed to achieve gauge

1 stitch marker
Yarn needle

I like to have a smaller, sharper needle at hand for working my lifted increases. It greatly reduces the stress on the yarn and my hands.

GAUGE

32 sts and 44 rnds = 4"/10 cm in stockinette stitch

PATTERN

Toe

Using an open provisional cast on, CO 28 (30, 32, 34, 38, X) sts.
Purl those stitches.

Set-up Row 1 (RS): Sl1, k26 (28, 30, 32, 36, X–2), m1L. Turn.
Set-up Row 2 (WS): Sl1, p26 (28, 30, 32, 36, X–2), m1P. Turn.

Shorter Short Row 1 (RS): Sl1, k25 (27, 29, 31, 35, X–3), m1L. Turn.
Shorter Short Row 2 (WS): Sl1, p24 (26, 28, 30, 34, X–4), m1P. Turn.

FOR A NARROW HEEL/TOE:

Continue in patt as set by the Shorter Short rows, working one less stitch on each row before making your increase, until you work a row where you purl 10 (10, 10, 12, 12, T) sts.

Then:
Turning Row 1 (RS): Sl1, k9 (9, 9, 11, 11, T–1), ssk, k1. Turn.
Turning Row 2 (WS): Sl1, p9 (9, 9, 11, 11, T–1), p2tog, p1. Turn.

Longer Short Row 1 (RS): Sl1, k10 (10, 10, 12, 12, T), ssk, k1. Turn.
Longer Short Row 2 (WS): Sl1, p11 (11, 11, 13, 13, T+1), p2tog, p1. Turn.

Proceed to "For All Styles."

FOR A MEDIUM HEEL/TOE:

Continue in patt as set by the Shorter Short rows, working one less stitch on each row before making your increase, until you work a row where you purl 14 (16, 16, 16, 20, T) sts.

FOR A WIDE HEEL/TOE:

Then:
Turning Row 1 (RS): Sl1, k13 (15, 15, 15, 19, T–1), ssk, k1. Turn.
Turning Row 2 (WS): Sl1, p13 (15, 15, 15, 19, T–1), p2tog, p1. Turn.

Longer Short Row 1 (RS): Sl1, k14 (16, 16, 16, 20, T), ssk, k1. Turn.
Longer Short Row 2 (WS): Sl1, p15, (17, 17, 17, 21, T+1), p2tog, p1. Turn.

Proceed to "For All Styles."

FOR A WIDE HEEL/TOE:

Continue in patt as set by the Shorter Short rows, working one less stitch on each row before making your increase, until you work a row where you purl 18 (20, 22, 22, 26, T) sts.

Then:
Turning Row 1 (RS): Sl1, k17 (19, 21, 21, 25, T–1), ssk, k1. Turn.
Turning Row 2 (WS): Sl1, p17 (19, 21, 21, 25, T–1), p2tog, p1. Turn.

WORKING OUT CUSTOM SIZING FOR ARITHMOPHOBIA, TOE UP

See page 49 for help with using this table. S must be divisible by 2.

For a narrow heel/toe: Determine S/6 sts. Round up or down to the nearest whole number. Let's call this T. This heel/toe will take S/3 rows to work before the first turning row. If you want to know how deep that is in inches or centimeters, divide S/3 by your row/round gauge.

For a medium heel/toe: Determine S/4 sts. Round up or down to the nearest whole number. Let's call this T. This heel/toe will take S/4 rows to work before the first turning row. If you want to know how deep that is in inches or centimeters, divide S/4 by your row/round gauge.

For a wide heel/toe: Determine S/3 sts. Round up or down to the nearest whole number. Let's call this T. This heel/toe will take S/6 rows to work before the first turning row. If you want to know how deep that is in inches or centimeters, divide S/6 by your row/round gauge. At some gauges, this heel/toe will be extremely short. It might work great for a toe, but it may really be too shallow for a heel. You might want to choose a medium or narrow heel.

Longer Short Row 1 (RS): Sl1, k18 (20, 22, 22, 26, T), ssk, k1. Turn.
Longer Short Row 2 (WS): Sl1, p19 (21, 23, 23, 27, T+1), p2tog, p1. Turn.

Proceed to "For All Styles."

FOR ALL STYLES

Repeat the longer short rows, working one more stitch on each row before making your decrease, until you have worked all of your stitches. You should have the original number of cast-on stitches on the needles, 28 (30, 32, 34, 38, X) sts. Pm for beginning of rnd. Knit across the live sts. Return sts from the provisional CO to needle and knit across them. Join to work in the round. 56 (60, 64, 68, 76, S) sts on the needles.

Foot

Work in stockinette stitch until the foot of the sock is as long as you want, less the length needed for the heel. How long is your heel? Measure the length of the toe; this is the length of your heel.

If you are working one style of toe and a different style of heel, direct measurement of your toe depth needs a slight modification. Take the number of stitches purled on Turning Row 2 for your toe, and subtract the number of stitches purled on the 2nd turning row for your planned heel. That's how many more (or fewer) rows your heel will have before the first turning row than your toe did. When measuring the toe to see how long your heel will be, simply add a marker that many rows deeper into the foot of the sock than your actual toe shaping (or shy of the final toe shaping row), and measure.

Heel

Work exactly as for the toe, starting with Set-up Row 1. When finished, join to work in the round on 56 (60, 64, 68, 76, S) stitches.

Leg

Work in stockinette stitch until the leg is 2"/5 cm shorter than desired.

Work in [k1, p1] ribbing for 2"/5 cm.

BO. I like Jeny's Surprisingly Stretchy Bind Off, but any bind off that is stretchy enough for the sock to get over the foot will work. Please see page 47 for more information about bind offs for toe-up socks.

Finishing

Weave in all ends and block gently.

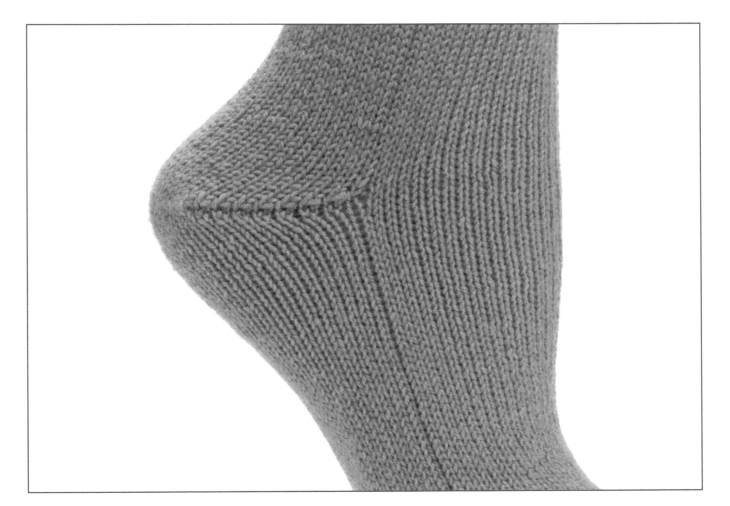

Adjoin

SIZES

Women's XS (Women's S, Women's M/Men's S, Women's L/Men's M, Men's L, Adjustable Size); shown in size Women's M

FINISHED MEASUREMENTS

Foot circumference: 7 (7½, 8, 8½, 9½, U)"/18 (19, 20.5, 21.5, 24, U) cm

Finished leg length: adjustable to fit
Finished foot length: adjustable to fit

MATERIALS

Simply Socks Yarn Company Simply Sock Yarn (80% superwash wool, 20% nylon; 175 yds/160m per 50g skein); color: #646 Blue Skies; 2 (2, 2, 2, 3, U) skeins

US#1 (2.25 mm) needles or size needed to achieve gauge

2 stitch markers
1 spare knitting needle of any type, same size as the working needles, for the Zigzag bind off
Yarn needle

GAUGE

32 sts and 44 rnds = 4"/10 cm in stockinette stitch

SPECIAL STITCHES

Adjoin Panel

(Worked over 13 sts in the round)
Follow either written instructions below or chart on following page.
Rnd 1: P1, k9, p1, k1, p1.
Rnd 2: P1, k3, cdd, k3, p1, m1R, k1, m1L, p1.

Rnd 3: P1, k7, p1, k3, p1.
Rnd 4: P1, k2, cdd, k2, p1, k1, m1R, k1, m1L, k1, p1.

Rnd 5: P1, k5, p1, k5, p1.
Rnd 6: P1, k1, cdd, k1, p1, k2, m1R, k1, m1L, k2, p1.

Rnd 7: P1, k3, p1, k7, p1.

Rnd 8: P1, cdd, p1, k3, m1R, k1, m1L, k3, p1.

Rnd 9: P1, k1, p1, k9, p1.
Rnd 10: P1, m1R, k1, m1L, p1, k3, cdd, k3, p1.

Rnd 11: P1, k3, p1, k7, p1.
Rnd 12: P1, k1, m1R, k1, m1L, k1, p1, k2, cdd, k2, p1.

Rnd 13: P1, k5, p1, k5, p1.
Rnd 14: P1, k2, m1R, k1, m1L, k2, p1, k1, cdd, k1, p1.

Rnd 15: P1, k7, p1, k3, p1.
Rnd 16: P1, k3, m1R, k1, m1L, k3, p1, cdd, p1.

Rep Rnds 1–16 for patt.

"ADJOIN" MEANS TO BE NEXT TO AND joined with, and is used sometimes when discussing boundaries between properties. It fits for this sock, which has a very different sort of heel shaping. Instead of wrapping around the heel with short rows, a flap is extended from the bottom of the sock to the back of the heel. It is then bound off. Stitches are picked up from the top of this flap to continue the leg. There is no gusset, but the depth of the heel shaping makes up for it.

If you haven't worked a toe-up sock before, never fear. This sock uses a "Training Wheel" toe that I designed with you in mind.

There is a very simple chart to follow, but I've also included stitch-by-stitch instructions for the stitch motif, if you prefer to work that way.

If the stitch motif doesn't appeal to you (I can see it wouldn't work for many men), you can ignore the instructions about it and instead simply work in stockinette for the foot and the front of the leg.

PATTERN

To work out your own custom sizing to use in the instructions that follow, see page 126.

Training Wheel Toe

This toe combines elements of the short-row toe and the wedge toe. I wrote it because a few of my friends expressed the desire to work toe-up socks, but were completely mystified at my instructions for starting a wedge toe.

Choose the shape of toe you want to use. (See the instructions for the Training Wheel Toe on page 40 if you need help deciding.)

Adjoin Panel Chart

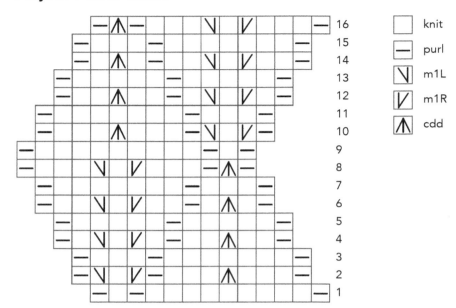

☐	knit
⊟	purl
⊻	m1L
⊽	m1R
⋀	cdd

See sidebar for instructions on how to work the toe for the Adjustable Size.

SHORT VERSION

Using an open provisional cast on, CO 10 (12, 12, 12, 14, –) sts.
Purl those sts.

Shorter Row 1 (RS): K9 (11, 11, 11, 13, –), m1L. Turn.
Shorter Row 2 (WS): Sl1, p8 (10, 10, 10, 12, –), m1P. Turn.

Turning Row 1 (RS): Sl1, k7 (9, 9, 9, 11, –), ssk, k1. Turn.
Turning Row 2 (WS): Sl1, p7 (9, 9, 9, 11, –), p2tog, p1. Turn.

You should have the original number of cast-on sts on the needle. Pm for beginning of rnd. Knit across the live sts. Place a second marker for center of rnd. Return sts from the provisional CO to needle. Join to work in the round. 20 (24, 24, 24, 28, –) sts.

Note: For this section, the beginning of the round is on the side of the sock.

Rnd 1: K1, m1L, knit to 1 st before marker, m1R, k2, m1L, knit to 1 st before end of rnd, m1R, k1. 4 sts increased.

Rep this rnd 3 (2, 3, 3, 4, U) more times, until you have 36 (36, 40, 40, 48, D) sts on the needles.

Next rnd: K1, m1L, knit to 1 st before marker, m1R, k2, m1L, knit to 1 st before end of rnd, m1R, k1. 4 sts increased.
Following rnd: Knit.
Rep these 2 rnds 4 (5, 5, 6, 6, U) more times, until you have 56 (60, 64, 68, 76, S) st on the needles.

MEDIUM VERSION

Using an open provisional cast on, CO 8 (8, 8, 8, 10, –) sts.
Purl those sts.

Shorter Row 1 (RS): K7 (7, 7, 7, 9, –), m1L. Turn.
Shorter Row 2 (WS): Sl1, p6 (6, 6, 6, 8, –), m1P. Turn.

Turning Row 1 (RS): Sl1, k5 (5, 5, 5, 7, –), ssk, k1. Turn.
Turning Row 2 (WS): Sl1, p5 (5, 5, 5, 7, –), p2tog, p1. Turn.

You should have the original number of cast-on sts on the needle. Pm for beginning of rnd. Knit across the live sts. Place a second marker for center

of rnd. Return sts from the provisional CO to needle. Join to work in the round. 16 (16, 16, 16, 20, U) sts.

Rnd 1: K1, m1L, knit to 1 st before marker, m1R, k2, m1L, knit to 1 st before end of rnd, m1R, k1. 4 sts increased.
Rep this rnd 2 (3, 3, 4, 4, U) more times, until you have 28 (32, 32, 36, 40, D) sts on the needles.

Next rnd: K1, m1L, knit to 1 st before marker, m1R, k2, m1L, knit to 1 st before end of rnd, m1R, k1. 4 sts increased.
Following rnd: Knit.
Rep these 2 rnds 6 (6, 7, 7, 8, –) more times, until you have 56 (60, 64, 68, 76, S) sts on the needles.

LONG VERSION

Using an open provisional cast on, CO 8 (8, 8, 8, 10, –) sts.
Purl those sts.

Shorter Row 1 (RS): K7 (7, 7, 7, 9, –), m1L. Turn.
Shorter Row 2 (WS): Sl1, p6 (6, 6, 6, 8, –), m1P. Turn.

Turning Row 1 (RS): Sl1, k5 (5, 5, 5, 7, –), ssk, k1. Turn.

Turning Row 2 (WS): Sl1, p5 (5, 5, 5, 7, –), p2tog, p1. Turn.

You should have the original number of cast-on sts on the needle. Pm for beginning of rnd. Knit across the live sts. Place a second marker for center of rnd. Return sts from the provisional CO to needle. Join to work in the round. 16 (16, 16, 16, 20, –) sts.

Rnd 1: K1, m1L, knit to 1 st before marker, m1R, k2, m1L, knit to 1 st before end of rnd, m1R, k1. 4 sts increased.
Rep this rnd 2 (3, 3, 4, 4, U) more times, until you have 28 (32, 32, 36, 40, D) sts on the needles.

Next rnd: K1, m1L, knit to 1 st before marker, m1R, k2, m1L, knit to 1 st before end of rnd, m1R, k1. 4 sts increased.
Knit 2 rnds even.
Rep these 3 rnds 6 (6, 7, 7, 8, –) more times, until you have 56 (60, 64, 68, 76, S) sts on the needles.

Foot

Remove center-of-rnd marker.
Set-up Rnd: K8 (9, 10, 11, 13, F) sts, pm, knit to end of rnd.

Begin working in patt as follows: Knit to marker, sm, work Adjoin panel, knit to end of rnd.

Work even in patt until foot measures 2½ (2¾, 3, 3, 3½, X/11)"/6.5 (7, 7.5, 7.5, 8.5, X/4.4) cm less than desired length. (The heel shaping takes 28 (30, 32, 34, 38, X) rows to work.)

Heel

To begin the heel, half the sts are put on hold for the instep. The heel sts are then worked flat alone.

Work 28 (30, 32, 34, 38, X) sts in patt then put them on waste yarn, a stitch holder, or simply leave them on the needles. Leave the stitch marker for the Adjoin panel in place. Write down the

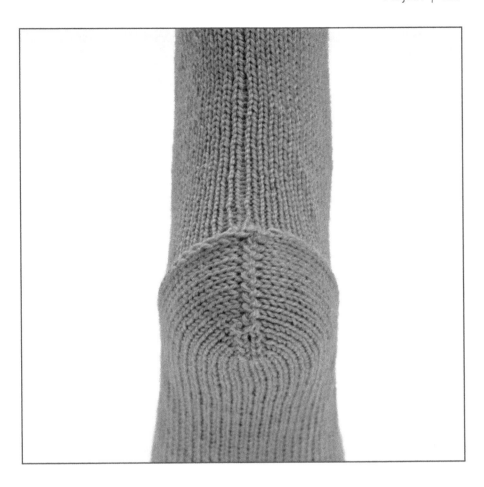

last round you worked for the Adjoin panel so you'll know where to resume after the heel.

Work the 28 (30, 32, 34, 38, X) heel sts back and forth as follows:

Row 1 (RS): Sl1, knit to end. Turn.
Row 2 (WS): Sl1, purl to end. Turn.
Work these 2 rows 9 (10, 11, 12, 13, J) times more.

Pm halfway across your heel sts—14 (15, 16, 17, 19, X/2) sts on each side of the marker.

Row 1 (RS): Sl1, knit to 2 sts before marker, k2tog, sm, ssk, knit to end. 2 sts decreased.
Row 2 (WS): Sl1, purl to end.
Rep these 2 rows 3 (3, 3, 3, 4, K) more times. 20 (22, 24, 26, 28, [X–2(K–1)]L) sts rem.

Next row (RS): Sl1, knit to 2 sts before marker, k2tog, sm, ssk, knit to end.
Turn to WS, sl1, purl to marker.

Fold the work with the wrong sides together and use a Zigzag bind off (see page) to close.

Pm for start of rnd, pick up and knit 1 stitch for every slipped-edge stitch along the top left side of the heel flap, work in patt across instep sts, pick up and knit 1 stitch for every slipped-edge stitch along the top right side of the heel flap. You should now have as many sts as you had on the foot. 56 (60, 64, 68, 76, S) sts total.

Leg and Bind Off

Resume working in patt as for foot: Knit to marker, sm, work next rnd of Adjoin panel, knit to end of rnd.

Work even in patt until leg measures 2"/5 cm less than desired length.

Work in [k1, p1] ribbing for 2"/5 cm.

WORKING OUT CUSTOM SIZING FOR ADJOIN

See page 49 for help with using this table. S must be divisible by 4.

Variable	How to calculate that variable	Write your result below
X	S/2	
A	X × 0.75 Round to nearest even number.	
B	X × 0.25 Round to nearest even number.	
Add A & B together and make sure they add up to X. If they don't, make A larger (and B smaller, if needed) until they do.		
J	(A / 2) − 1	
K	(B / 2) − 1	
L	X − (2 × K) − 2	
D	S × 0.6 Round to multiple of 4.	
C	For Short Toe: (S × 0.15) + 2 Round to nearest even number. For Medium and Long Toes: (S × 0.1) + 2 Round to nearest even number.	
F	(X − 12) / 2 If this is not a whole number, round down. If you are leaving out the lace pattern, you do not need to calculate F.	

The toe instructions in this pattern work for all versions of the toe in the adjustable size. Follow them through the end of the second turning row, then continue with the set that applies to your toe.

Using an open provisional cast on, CO C sts.
Purl those sts.

Shorter Row 1: Knit to 1 st from end, m1L. Turn.
Shorter Row 2: Sl1, purl to 1 st from end, m1P. Turn.

Turning Row 1: Sl1, knit 1 fewer st than you purled the row before, ssk, k1. Turn.
Turning Row 2: Sl1, purl the same number of sts as you knit the row before, p2tog, p1. Turn.

BO. I like Jeny's Surprisingly Stretchy Bind Off, but any bind off that is stretchy enough for the sock to get over the foot will work. Please see page 47 for more information about bind offs for toe-up socks.

Finishing

Weave in all ends and block gently.

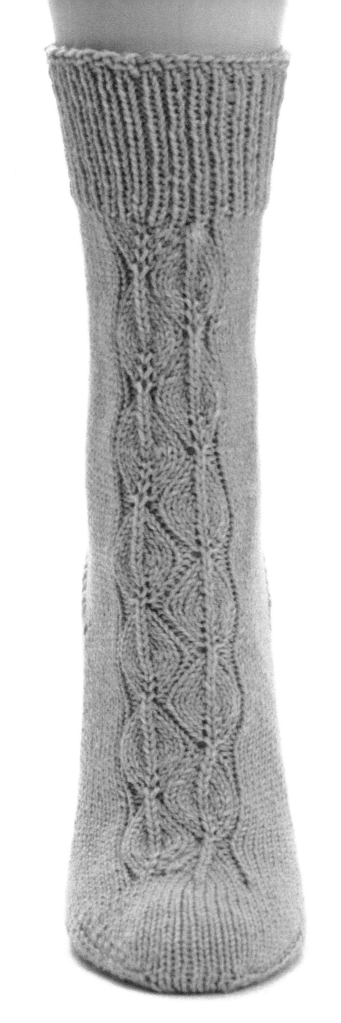

Resources

approx	approximately
BO	bind off
cdd	centered double decrease: slip 2 sts as if to k2tog, k1, pass 2 slipped sts over
CO	cast on
k	knit
k2tog	right-leaning decrease: knit 2 sts together as one
kfb	knit into front and back of a single stitch (increase)
m1L	use tip of LH needle to lift strand between sts from front to back; knit through the back loop (increase)
m1P	use tip of LH needle to lift strand between sts from back to front; purl loop (increase)
m1PR	use tip of LH needle to lift strand between sts from front to back; purl through the back loop (increase)
m1R	bring tip of LH needle under strand between sts from back to front; knit loop (increase)
p	purl
p2tog	purl 2 sts together as one
patt	pattern
pm	place marker
rep	repeat
rnd(s)	round(s)
RS	right side (public side)
sl	slip
sm	slip marker
ssk	left-leaning decrease: slip 2 sts knitwise one at a time, then knit them together through the back loop
st(s)	stitches
WS	wrong side (private side)

Abbreviations

Emily Ocker's Circular Beginning

A crochet hook makes this process much easier. Make a loop of yarn and let the short end hang down. Let's call that the "main loop." Draw a loop through the main loop, then draw another loop through the loop you just made. Repeat for each stitch to be cast on. After you have worked your main piece, pull on the loose end to tighten the loop and close the circle.

Provisional Cast On

Either watch my video tutorial online at <vimeo.com/101286979>, or follow the photographed steps below:

Casting on this way takes sets of four motions, but each set makes two stitches.

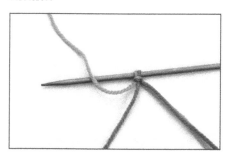

If you don't already have other stitches to anchor your strands, tie slip knots in each one to start. For the example pictured above, the green yarn is the bottom strand, while the blue one is the top strand. The green strand can later be pulled out, leaving live stitches. The first few times you try this cast on, I recommend using two colors. Two colors makes it infinitely easier to see when you've made a mistake.

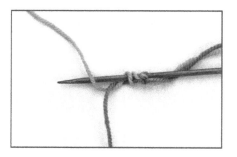

Wrap the top strand around the bottom of the needle, from the front to the back (as above).

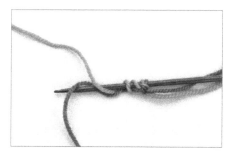

Wrap the bottom strand around the top of the needle, from the back to the front (as above).

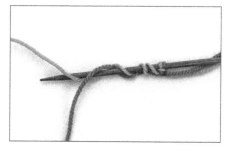

Catch the top strand with the needle, from the back to the front (as above).

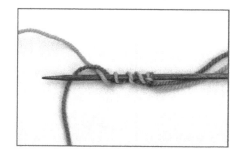

Bring the bottom strand around the top of the needle, from the front to the back, to secure the top strand (as above)—4 stitches cast on.

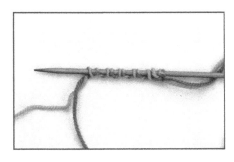

The photo above shows 10 stitches cast on. What might appear to be the first two are just the slip knots, which should be pulled off the needle as soon as is practical.

Strap Closure

(worked over 4 stitches)

Start with k1, ssk. Turn.

Row 1: Sl1, p2, p2tog. Turn.
Row 2: Sl1, k2, ssk. Turn.

Repeat these 2 (very short) rows until 8 stitches remain. Graft the working stitches and the other 4 stitches together. The strap closure can be as narrow or wide as you like, although I'm not sure how one would make it smaller than 2 stitches across.

Preventing/Closing Gusset Gaps

In the photo above, the stitches have been picked up for the gusset, and we are ready to pick up an extra stitch or two to close any gaps.

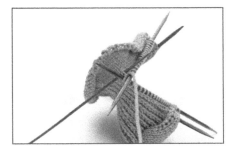

The smaller needle above (the needle crossing from bottom left to top right) shows where the next stitch should be picked up.

On the other side, starting from the top of the gusset, two "extra" stitches need to be added. The tip of the needle (above) shows the pick-up position for the first of those stitches.

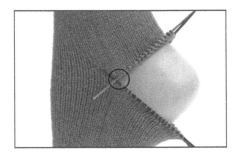

The final image above shows heel stitches ready to be worked on an after-thought heel. The black circle outlines the two "ear" stitches, which could be switched to tighten up the area and prevent a gap.

Zigzag Bind Off

Used to join two sets of live stitches. Designate one side of the heel stitches as side 1 and the other as side 2.

With a spare needle, k1 from side 1, p1 from side 2. Pass the 1st stitch over the 2nd stitch on your spare needle.

Then, repeat as follows until all stitches are bound off:
Row 1: K1 from side 1, pass the 1st stitch over the 2nd stitch on your spare needle.
Row 2: P1 from side 2, pass the 1st stitch over the 2nd stitch on your spare needle.

About the Yarn: Simply Socks Yarn Company

ALLISON VAN ZANDT opened Simply Socks Yarn Company as an online business in 2005. She opened her showroom in Fort Wayne in August of 2011 in a former post office that was built in the late 1940s in a vibrant neighborhood. In one fell swoop, she saved a historic building and allowed knitters to experience over five tons of sock yarn spread out over 3,500 square feet.

Her shop is a beacon of inspiration, but so is Allison, herself. She believed in this book even before I did, and she backed it up with the yarn to prove it. Simply Sock Yarn Solids comes in 66 gorgeous hand-dyed solid and semi-solid colors, each hand-picked by Allison. I used ten different colors for the designs in this book.

Not just a pretty face, this yarn is hard-wearing and fun to knit, with great stitch definition.

Be on the lookout for her new line of self-striping yarns, Poste Yarn. Hand-dyed in the back room of the shop by artisan and shop manager Heather Terrill, they sell out fast!

Bibliography

Anonymous. *The Ladies' Work-Table Book*. London: 1850.
<pdf.library.soton.ac.uk/WSA_open_access/00376344.pdf>

Branchardiere, Mlle. Riego de la. *The Abergeldie Winter Book*. London: Simpkin, Marshall and Co., 1867.
<pdf.library.soton.ac.uk/WSA_open_access/00376326.pdf>

Bryson, Bill. *At Home: A Short History of Private Life*. Transworld Digital, 2010, Kindle edition.

Bush, Nancy. *Folk Socks*. Loveland, Colorado: Interweave Press, 1994.

Cupples, George Mrs. *The Stocking-Knitter's Manual: A Handy Book for the Work-Table*. Edinburgh: Johnstone, Hunter and Co., c. 1870.
<pdf.library.soton.ac.uk/WSA_open_access/00393973.pdf>

Gaugain, Jane. *The Lady's Assistant for Executing Useful and Fancy Designs in Knitting, Netting, and Crochet Work*. Edinburgh: 1840.
An electronic version was downloaded for research: <archive.org/details/TheLadysAssistantForExecutingUsefulAndFancyDesignsInKnitting>

Gibson-Roberts, Priscilla. *Ethnic Socks & Stockings: A Compendium of Eastern Design and Technique*. Sioux Falls: XRX, 1995.

Gibson-Roberts, Priscilla. *Simple Socks Plain and Fancy*. Cedaredge: Nomad Press, 2001.

Mee, Cornelia. *Exercises in Knitting*. Project Gutenberg ePub edition. Originally published in 1846.
<archive.org/details/exercisesinknitt21032gut>

Misegades, Katherine. *... And a Time to Knit Stockings*. Self-published reprint, 2007.
<www.atimetoknit.com/d_k_ATTK.html>

Parkes, Clara. *The Knitter's Book of Socks*. New York: Potter Craft, 2011.

Rutt, Richard. *A History of Handknitting*. Loveland, Colorado: Interweave Press, 2003. [Reprint of 1987 publication by London: B. T. Batsford.]

Smith, Andi. *Big Foot Knits*. Cleveland: Cooperative Press, 2013.

Zilboorg, Anna. *Fancy Feet: Traditional Knitting Patterns of Turkey*. Asheville, NC: Lark Books, 1994.

About Lara Neel

photo courtesy of Knitty.com

Lara Neel published over 150 free patterns in three years for the Math4Knitters, Crafty Living blog and podcast. Now, when she's not dreaming of more books, she's offering select, test-knit (and/or tech-edited) patterns for sale.

Her work has also appeared in *Knit Edge*, Petite Purls, The Ennea Collective, and Knitty. The easiest way to reach her is on Ravelry or her blog, math4knitters.blogspot.com. She is Math4Knitters. She would love to hear from you.

Acknowledgments

Every book is a collaboration among many people, and this one is no different. Many people helped me, intentionally. Others helped me in other ways. I hope I don't forget to thank anyone, but I know I will.

To my mom and dad, for always supporting me and listening, even when I talk about physics or sock heels.

To my sister, Lisa, and her growing family. Thanks for being my favorite knitwear models of all time.

To my partner, Dee, for building a life so full of joy I couldn't even have hoped or wished for it.

To the listeners and readers of Math4Knitters and Math4Knitters, Crafty Living, especially the ones who put up with my early efforts at pattern writing.

To the knitters who sacrificed their knitting time and, sometimes, sanity, to test out my designs: Ann P. Bradley, Jodie Emerick, Kandice Force-Swanner, Kathryn Haines, Chevas Hefflinger, Lisa Japko, Gina Kostoff, Dora Lenchuk, Heather Lytle, Joyce McCartney, Natalie McLaughlin, Anna Mieszkowska, Cindy Mizell, Kaia Nelson, Beth Patterson, Kristin Strong, Lori Veteto, Michelle Walden, and Rebecca Wood.

To Shannon Okey and all of the wonderful people that make Cooperative Press work. I *really* couldn't have done it without you.

Last but really, really not least, to Kate Atherley and Eleanor Dixon for being generally awesome, gentle, kind, and good at helping me untangle myself.

About Cooperative Press

COOPERATIVE PRESS (formerly anezka media) was founded in 2007 by Shannon Okey, a voracious reader as well as writer and editor, who had been doing freelance acquisitions work, introducing authors with projects she believed in to editors at various publishers.

Although working with traditional publishers can be very rewarding, there are some books that fly under their radar. They're too avant-garde, or the marketing department doesn't know how to sell them, or they don't think they'll sell 50,000 copies in a year.

5,000 or 50,000. Does the book matter to that 5,000? Then it should be published.

In 2009, Cooperative Press changed its named to reflect the relationships we have developed with authors working on books. We work together to put out the best quality books we can and share in the proceeds accordingly.

Thank you for supporting independent publishers and authors.

Join our mailing list for information on upcoming books!

WWW.COOPERATIVEPRESS.COM

9 781937 513634